Recovery Relationship Anxiety and Overthinking

(2 Books in 1)

Stop Being Anxious and Needy. Build Confidence,
Self-Esteem and Break Negative Spirals in
Relationships

Linda Hill

i

Table of Contents

Book #1: Anxious Attachment Recovery...................... 1

Introduction.. 3

Chapter 1: Attachment Styles - Our Blueprint to Intimacy.......... 5

What is an Attachment Style? 6

The Attachment Styles 8

Secure Attachment Style 10

Anxious Attachment Style... 12

Avoidant Attachment Style 15

How Attachment Styles are formed................................ 17

The Causes for an Insecure Attachment........................... 19

The Power of Connection 20

Inside the Mind of an Infant.. 22

The Stages of Attachment Development........................... 23

What goes into a Child's Attachment? 25

Theories on Attachment Formation................................. 26

Chapter 2: How Attachment Styles Affect Relationships **29**

Secure Attachment Style 30

Anxious Attachment Style 31

Avoidant Attachment Style 34

Chapter 3: The Anxious Attachment Style **36**

How Anxious Attachment Styles are Created 37

Which Children Are at the Greatest Risk? 39

Signs of Anxious Attachment 40

Chapter 4: The Anxious Attachment Style in Relationships **44**

The Dance of Opposites 47

The Origins of Anxious and Avoidant Dance 48

Relationships: The Mirrors to Our Concealments 50

The Anxious Attachment Style in the WorkPlace 52

Chapter 5: How to Cope with Your Anxious Attachment Style . **54**

Bringing Awareness to Anxious Attachment 55

Modern Technology as a Trigger 58

Triggered Behaviors 59

How to Handle Triggers in Yourself 60

Chapter 6: The Anxious Attachment Style, Partners, and Dating **70**

Dating and Anxious Attachment Style 70

Current Relationships and the Anxious Attachment Style 72

Make Use of Your Support System 75

What You Can Do for an Anxiously Attached Partner................................77

What to do if you are in an Anxious and Avoidant Relationship 80

Chapter 7: Research on the Anxious Attachment Style 82

Gratitude: A New Way to Deal with Anxious Attachment?.....................82

The Research: It Does Not Take Much!..84

Can You Change Your Attachment Style? 88

Image of Self and Others..89

Chapter 8: Guided Meditations and Affirmations...................... 92

About Meditation...92

What is Guided Meditation? 93

Guided Meditation: Before Getting Started 94

Mindfulness of the Sensations of the Body.................................95

Guided Meditation for Relaxing...96

Guided Meditation for Managing Your Emotions............................102

Guided Meditation for Transforming your Emotions.........................111

Guided Visualization 116

Guided Meditations for Relationships.....................................117

Guided Meditation for Relationship Success 126

Affirmations 132

How Affirmations Work..132

How to Use Affirmations..133

Final Words 161

Book #2: Crush Negative Thoughts.............163

Introduction 165

Understanding Overthinking 166

Your Brain and Emotions 170

Before Continuing 173

Chapter 1: Overthinking Is the Root of It All 182

Thinking About Thinking........................ 183

Signs You Are an Overthinker 185

Journaling........................ 198

Chapter 2: The Obsessions And Anxieties Of An Overthinker.199

Obsessions 200

Anxiety........................202

How It Affects Your Life........................204

Journal........................214

Chapter 3: Eliminate Through Awareness 216

Why You Need It 217

Awareness and Overthinking........................217

Implementing Awareness 218

Journal........................225

Chapter 4: The Quickest Way to Stop Overthinking 227

Cognitive Replacement 227

Self-Awareness and Hindsight...229

Focus on What Can Go Right...232

The Right Perspective..233

Being Aware of Your Emotions...235

Journaling..236

Chapter 5: Dump All Negative Thinking...............................238

The Negativity Cycle...239

Begin the Dump..241

The Actual Steps...249

Summary...252

Journal..254

Chapter 6: Life-Changing Practices to Stop Overthinking.......255

Practices to Stop Overthinking Forever...................................255

Journal..266

Conclusion 267

Thank You 271

Book #1

Anxious Attachment Recovery

Go From Being Clingy to Confident &
Secure in Your Relationships

Introduction

There is a metaphor that I once heard and it goes something like this: a moth is attracted to a flame, and each time it circles the flame, it gets closer to it. There comes a point when the moth gets too close and singes its wings. Wounded, the moth flies off. In a way, this describes the relationships of many people.

Have you ever experienced a relationship where your partner became too clingy, or required constant reassurance? On the other hand, perhaps this describes you. When I was much younger, I felt the most important thing was for me to be in a relationship.

Unfortunately, my relationships at that time did not last long. I would meet someone who I was interested in and we would start dating. But the more attracted I felt, the more insecure I felt. I kept anticipating that they would lose interest in me.

Sure enough, that is what occurred. However, I now believe they lost interest in me because I grew increasingly insecure when I was around them. The qualities that initially caused them to become interested in me would gradually fade away as my insecurities were exposed.

Today, I understand why I did what I did back then. I also understand that this period in my life was necessary to become who I am today. At that time, my interactions in relationships were governed by my attachment style. I am referring to anxious attachment style.

According to a 1987 study at the University of Denver, approximately 20% of the population have an anxious attachment style. This means that two out of 10 people you enter a relationship with will be anxious regarding emotional intimacy. This book will explore what an anxious attachment style is, how it is formed, what triggers this attachment style, and how you can cope with it. Whether it is you or a partner that has an anxious attachment style, understanding and being informed are the keys to moving beyond it.

CHAPTER 1

Attachment Styles - Our Blueprint to Intimacy

As a young adult, I was insecure regarding relationships, especially when dating men. If I was sincerely interested in a man, I often feared he would lose interest in me. This fear stemmed from the belief that I was not good enough. As a result, I was very reactive. I was honed in on what I perceived were expressions of disappointment or disapproval. In those moments, I felt that I had blown it and that they were losing interest in me.

When I was in my mid-twenties, I moved to Texas from California due to a job offer I had received. I was raised in California, and this was my first time moving to a new state. I did not know anyone in Texas, so I spent most of my time alone.

Because of this, I did not feel judged or that I had to impress anyone. Instead, I spent a lot of time in self-reflection, and I started meditating. I believe this experience was my turning point and had a transformative effect on me. I developed a greater appreciation for myself

In time, I started dating again; however, this time, it felt different. I felt more relaxed and confident. I did not panic if I felt that I was being judged or disapproved of. I realized that a shift had occurred in me. No longer did I place my self-worth in the hands of others. Instead, my sense of self-worth was embraced from within. I had learned to accept myself for who I was and became comfortable in my own skin. I learned that I was good enough just being me. I did not know it then, but I had moved beyond the influence of my anxious attachment style.

What is an Attachment Style?

So, what is an attachment style? An attachment style is the kind of bond we form with others. To better understand this, it is helpful to look at an experiment that psychologist Harry Harlow did in 1930. Before going further, I need to state that I find Harlow's experiment unethical, but it provides important insight into attachment styles.

In the experiment, Harlow separated infant rhesus monkeys from their mothers. Harlow constructed two different kinds of surrogate mothers. The first surrogate was made of metal but had an artificial nipple from which the infant monkeys could get milk. The second surrogate was covered with soft and fluffy material; however, it did not provide food.

When the baby monkeys were hungry, they went to the first surrogate. However, they would go to the second one when they sought comfort. The second surrogate provided the infant monkeys with a sense of security.

These monkeys were curious and explored their surroundings. If they felt unsure, they would return to their surrogate. However, when the infants were placed in a new environment without their surrogate, they would not explore. Instead, they would rock back and forth on the floor and suck their thumb.

Harlow's experiment showed that the monkeys' need for comfort was just as important as their need for food. With the second surrogate, the infant monkeys could build trust and confidence.

In 1969, psychoanalyst John Bowlby wrote about his theory of attachments in humans. Bowlby believed that attachments were an instinctive emotional connection that promoted the exchange of care, comfort, and pleasure. From an evolutionary standpoint, Bowlby believed that attachments are necessary for our survival as a species.

We form attachments with our primary caregiver from the moment of our birth until around three years of age. The quality of the attachments that we form determines our ability to trust others and our level of self-confidence.

As with the baby monkeys, if we meet our emotional needs, we develop the confidence to explore the unfamiliar and trust others. However, when we do not get our emotional needs met, we may have challenges in being able to trust or explore the unknown. Research has identified four different styles of attachment:

- Secure attachments

- Anxious attachments

- Avoidant attachments

- Disorganized attachments

These attachment styles will be discussed in detail in a later chapter. For now, secure attachments lead to trust in others and confidence within ourselves. The remaining attachments are based on fear and are collectively known as insecure attachments. They lead to anxiousness and mistrust of others. It is for this reason that knowing your attachment style is important.

The type of attachment that we develop as young children may remain with us into adulthood, and influence our interactions within our adult relationships, especially intimate ones. The following are examples:

1. Secure Style: You feel secure in your own space and can be open and supportive toward your partner.

2. Anxious Style: You do not trust your partner's feelings for you and need continuous reassurance from them.

3. Avoidant Style: You have trouble opening up or showing your emotions.

4. Disorganized Style: You do not trust your partner or others. You either push people away or have an unhealthy need for closeness.

It is estimated that 56% of the population has the secure style, 20% exhibit the anxious style, 23% the avoidant style, and 1% the disorganized style.

The Attachment Styles

In the 1970s, Ainsworth conducted a landmark study known as the Strange Situation Study. In the study, she looked at how children between 12-18 months responded to their mother leaving them alone for brief moments and then returning.

The experiment began with the mother and child being in a room alone.

Ainsworth looked to see if the child would explore the room under their mother's supervision. Afterward, a stranger would enter the room, talk to the mother, and approach the child. The mother would then leave the room but return shortly to comfort her child.

Ainsworth used her observations of the children to create the three major attachment styles: secure attachment, anxious attachment, and avoidant attachment. According to attachment theory, the memory of our connection to our primary caregivers is retained into adulthood, though we may be unconscious of it. In adulthood, we seek out partners that reflect that connection.

The attachment styles represent the quality of those connections. Take a moment to consider which of the following statements you most identify with:

1. It is easy for me to feel connected to others. I am willing to depend on those I feel close to, as I am comfortable with having them depend on me.

2. I am not satisfied with the level of closeness in my relationships. I feel others are not as close to me as I would like. I am frequently concerned that my partner does not really love me, or that they would rather not be with me.

3. I am uncomfortable getting close to others and feel uncomfortable when they try to get close to me. I have experienced situations where others wanted me to become more intimate than I am comfortable with.

These three statements characterize the three styles of attachment. The fourth attachment style, disorganized attachment, is a blend of the anxious and avoidant styles. Because of this fact, along with it being a rarity, it will not be discussed in this program. The following is a more detailed look at the three styles:

Secure Attachment Style

It is easy for me to feel connected to others. I am willing to depend on those I feel close to, as I am comfortable with having them depend on me.

You may have a secure attachment style if you identify with this statement. This attachment style leads to healthy and long-lasting relationships and is forged by having a secure relationship with one's primary caregiver. Developing a secure attachment style in a child does not require that the parent or caregiver be perfect.

No parent can be fully in tune with their child's needs 24 hours a day. These parents may misinterpret their child's nonverbal cues, but they continue trying different things until they meet their needs. Because the child knows they are supported, they can freely express their need for validation or reassurance without fearing punishment.

In Ainsworth's experiment, she found that children who had a secure attachment showed the following:

- They freely explored the room while their mother was there.

- They sought their mother's comfort when they were scared or unsure.

- When their mother returned to the room, they greeted her with positive emotions.

- They preferred being with their mother than with a stranger.

Early interactions with their primary caregiver make the child feel safe, understood, and valued. The child feels this way because their primary caregiver is emotionally available to them. Further, their primary caregiver is self-aware of their own emotions and behavior. The child learns from the primary caregiver and models their behaviors. You probably have a secure attachment style if you:

- Can regulate your emotions.

- Readily trust others.

- Can communicate effectively.

- Can ask for emotional support.

- Are comfortable being alone.

- Are comfortable in close relationships.

- Can self-reflect on your relationships.

- Connect easily with others.

- Can manage conflicts.

- Have good self-esteem.

- Are emotionally available.

As a result, those who carry their secure attachment style into adulthood are emotionally secure and can navigate relationships healthily. They are trusting, loving, and emotionally supportive toward their partners.

Anxious Attachment Style

I am not satisfied with the level of closeness in my relationships. I feel others are not as close to me as I would like. I am frequently concerned that my partner does not really love me or that they would rather not be with me.

You may have an anxious attachment style if you identify with this statement. This attachment style occurs when the child learns they cannot depend on their primary caregiver to meet their comfort needs. Insecure attachment styles result from inconsistent parenting and not being attuned to the child's needs.

The child does not feel a sense of security with their primary caregiver. Inconsistent parenting creates confusion for the child. In Ainsworth's experiment, children with an anxious attachment style exhibited high distress when the mother left the room.

Inconsistencies in parenting are not the only way anxious attachment styles can occur. The experience of traumatic events can also be a cause. Another cause can be if parents are overprotective of a child. In this case, the child may pick up on their parents' anxiety and become fearful.

Those with an anxious attachment style may have had a primary caregiver who:

- Was inconsistent in comforting their child. Sometimes they may have coddled the child, while other times were indifferent or detached.

- Was easily overwhelmed.

- Alternated between being attentive toward the child and pushing them away.

- Made the child feel responsible for how they felt. It is believed that this kind of parenting can lead the child to become codependent later in life. They grow up believing they are responsible for other people's feelings.

Signs that you may have the anxious attachment style include:

- Being codependent

- Strong fears of rejection

- A dependency on your partner for validation or to make you feel better emotionally

- Having clingy tendencies

- Overly sensitive to criticism

- A need for validation from others

- Problems with jealousy

- You have difficulty being alone

- Low self-esteem

- Feeling unworthy of love

- A strong fear of abandonment

- Issues with trust

In relationships, the anxious attachment style can show up as the following:

- The person with this style does not feel worthy of being loved and needs continuous validation from their partner.

- They believe that they are responsible for the challenges in the relationship.

- They can be intensely jealous.

- Their low self-esteem causes them to distrust their partner.

- They may be overly sensitive to their partner's behaviors and emotions and jump to conclusions about their partner's intent.

All of these signs come from a strong fear of being abandoned. Though the person may want an intimate relationship, their fear of abandonment prevents them from developing the relationship they desire. Those with this attachment style may focus on their partner's needs while dismissing their own.

Traits of anxious attachment styles can also develop in adults. If someone experiences inconsistent behavior from their partner, they can develop traits of this style. If a partner is inconsistent in expressing affection, or if they are emotionally abusive, it can lead to the other person developing anxiety or insecurity about the relationship. An example of this is abusive relationships.

If a person is in a relationship with a partner who constantly tells them they are incompetent or unintelligent, that person may eventually believe it. This belief may cause them to cling to their partner. They will rely on their partner to care for them because they do not feel they can make it on their own.

Avoidant Attachment Style

I am uncomfortable getting close to others and get uncomfortable when they try to get close to me. I have experienced situations where others wanted me to become more intimate than I am comfortable with.

Those with an avoidant attachment style cannot form long-term relationships as they are challenged by a fear of emotional and physical intimacy. This attachment style is found in children who had primary caregivers that were strict, emotionally unavailable, or absent. As children, these individuals may have experienced:

- Not being supported and left to fend for themselves.

- They were expected to be independent before they were ready to be.

- Punished for depending on their primary caregivers.

- They were rejected by their primary caregivers when they expressed their emotions or needs.

- Their basic needs were not given high priority.

While such primary caregivers may have behaved this way due to outright neglect, others may have been overwhelmed with other responsibilities. Either way, these children grew up to be strongly independent. They are uncomfortable looking toward others to get their needs met, or for support.

You may have an avoidant attachment style if:

- You continuously avoid emotional or physical intimacy.

- You are fiercely independent.

- You avoid expressing your feelings.

- You have a dismissive attitude toward others.

- You are unable to trust others.

- You feel anxious when others try to get close to you.

- You avoid interacting with others.

- You believe that you do not need other people.

- You have commitment issues.

In relationships, those who have this attachment style keep their distance. Because they do not desire emotional intimacy, they never develop relationships where emotional depth is experienced.

The partners of those with avoidant attachment commonly feel that they do not know them and feel stone-walled when the other person feels the relationship is becoming too serious. In Ainsworth's experiment, children with the avoidant attachment style showed no preference between their mother and the stranger. Further, they did not seek out comfort from their mothers.

How Attachment Styles are formed

Attachment styles can be thought of as the lasting emotional connection between two individuals. In this relationship, each individual seeks the other for security and closeness.

In adult-child relationships, attachment is demonstrated by the adult responding to the child's needs sensitively and appropriately. Additionally, attachment by the child is formed not to the adult who spends the most time with them, but rather by the adult that meets more of the child's needs.

The meeting of the needs of the child is the essence of attachment theory. More specifically, the attachment theory centers on the need for security by the child. The child needs to be able to find security when it feels threatened or unsure.

One of the early founders of the attachment theory was psychoanalyst John Bowlby. In 1969, Bowlby published his theories on the subject. Bowlby believed that attachments were essential for the survival of our species because they were an emotional connection that caused babies to remain close to their mothers. From this emotional connection, Bowlby concluded that the following characteristics of attachment are meaningful to babies in their relationships with their caregivers or parents:

Closeness: Babies desire to stay close to those with whom they have formed attachments.

Safety: Babies look to their primary caregiver for safety when they are feeling unsure or fearful.

Comfort: By being a source of comfort, the primary caregiver creates the opportunity for babies to develop the confidence they need to explore their surrounding environment.

Separation Anxiety: Because of their dependency on their primary caregivers, babies experience fear when they are not around.

If the primary caregiver to the child is attentive to the child's needs, then the child learns to associate the primary caregiver with being a dependable source for getting their emotional needs met. They will develop what is known as a secure attachment style.

However, if the primary caregiver is not attentive to the child's needs, the child learns they cannot depend on their primary caregiver to meet their needs. The child will develop what is known as an insecure attachment style. The child's ability or inability to trust their primary caregiver to meet their needs may carry over into adulthood. When this happens, the person's childhood experience will be projected onto adult relationships.

If the child can trust their primary care giver in meeting their needs, they will more likely be able to trust their partners when they are adults. They will be able to experience emotional intimacy with them. However, if the child learns they cannot trust their primary caregiver to meet their emotional needs, they will have difficulty trusting their partners. Unless a conscious effort is made to change, they will be unable to experience emotional intimacy with their partners.

As with the baby monkeys, if we meet our emotional needs, we develop the confidence to explore the unfamiliar and trust others. However, when we do not get our emotional needs met, we may have challenges in being able to trust or explore the unknown.

The Causes for an Insecure Attachment

There are a number of factors that can lead to young children developing an insecure attachment style:

- The primary caregiver was young or inexperienced.

- The primary caregiver suffered from depression.

- The primary caregiver was addicted to drugs or alcohol.

- The primary caregiver or child experienced trauma.

- The child experienced physical neglect, such as improper nutrition, inadequate exercise, or unaddressed medical issues.

- The child experienced emotional abuse or neglect. Examples of this are the primary caregiver did not provide emotional attention to the child, did not attempt to understand the child's feelings, or was verbally abusive toward the child.

- The child experienced physical or sexual abuse.

- The child experienced separation from the primary caregiver due to divorce, adoption, illness, or death.

- The child lacked consistency in a primary caregiver figure. An example of this would be a child who experiences a succession of daycare staff or nannies.

- The child did not experience stability in placements. One example is a child who experiences constant change in their environment, such as moving from foster home to foster home.

In the early 21ˢᵗ century, the National Research Council and the Institute of Medicine's Committee on Integrating the Science of Early Childhood Development came to a conclusion that would shape its policies and practices. The conclusion was: "Children grow and thrive in the context of close and dependable relationships that provide love and nurturance, security, responsive interaction, and encouragement for exploration. Development is disrupted without at least one such relationship, and the consequences can be severe and long-lasting."

The Power of Connection

The most fundamental premise of attachment theory is that a child's fear is reduced when they are in proximity to the person with whom they have formed an attachment. What creates trust in the child is the child's perception of the availability of the person to be there to comfort them and make them feel safe.

When a child believes that their caregiver is both available and responsive to them, they can determine whether or not they can handle a perceived threat. If they feel they are capable, they will feel less anxiety and fear.

The body of research in attachment theory also shows that infants can receive complex information about the social interactions they observe. The information that is being referred to is both social and emotional in nature. In other words, infants can determine if the interactions they witness are caring or adversarial.

Studies using puppets showed that infants could identify whether the puppets' relationship was supportive and helpful or if it was hindering.

The infants showed a preference for those puppets that were helpful toward others. The infants did this because they already knew how the puppets should behave from previous observations modeling cooperative behavior.

The study demonstrated that infants could determine how the adults in their world behave toward each other. The infants then responded to the adults accordingly through their emotions and behaviors.

For children to feel that they have someone who they can depend upon for security not only has an emotional and behavioral effect on them, but it also can have a physiological effect, as demonstrated in a 1970s experiment. It was discovered that there is a physiological response in infant rats separated from their mothers. When the rat pups were separated from their mother, they demonstrated multiple changes in their physiological and behavioral levels. Body temperature, heart rate, food intake, and willingness to explore were all affected.

What was interesting is that not all the rat pups responded in the same way. Those rat pups that received the most attention from their mothers (in the form of maternal licking, grooming, and optimal nursing position) were least affected by being separated from their mothers. They also explored more than the other pups. The pups' development was tracked over time, and these differences in response to maternal separation were found to be maintained into adulthood.

Attachment research conducted in 1996 revealed that toddlers with an anxious attachment style had elevated cortical levels, a stress hormone when introduced to novel stimuli. The rise in cortical levels was also seen when mothers stopped interacting emotionally with their children. These same results were found with children from violent homes, even when they were not directly exposed to the violence.

All evidence from the research points to the same thing. For healthy development, children need a caregiver that provides them with a sense of security, and they need to feel that they can depend on that security when needed.

Internal Working Model of Attachment:

Inside the Mind of an Infant

From the time it is born, a child gains experiences from its interactions with its primary caregiver. It is from these experiences that a mental representation is formed. In attachment theory, these mental representations are known as internal working models of attachment (IWM). IWMs influence how children interact and form relationships with others. The child's expectations when interacting with others and forming relationships are based on their IWM.

A child's IWM is like a GPS or internal guidance system. It lays down the path for how the child will respond emotionally and behaviorally to others. This pathway can endure throughout the child's lifetime if there is no conscious decision by the person to change to a more empowering way of interacting with others and themselves.

The challenge is that these IWMs operate beyond our conscious awareness, which is why changing them is difficult. If not consciously addressed by the person, or if there are no intervening events in the person's life, their IWM will remain operative throughout their lives. For this reason, the quality of the parent-child relationship in the early stages of life is a good predictor of the child's relationships when they become adults.

It is from these IWMs that the attachment styles are based. Those with a secure attachment style will have a positive image of themselves and others and are comfortable with closeness and intimacy. Studies show that children who have formed a secure attachment style by age one are more likely to have positive relationships with others besides their parents. They are more likely to have positive relationships with their peers and teachers as well.

Unless there is some form of intervention, IWMs can become intergenerational. Children with a secure attachment style are more likely to pass on the secure attachment style to their own kids when they become parents.

Those with an anxious attachment style will have a negative image of themselves but a positive view of others. These people will fear intimacy and have a fear of abandonment. As parents, they are more likely to be abusive and create anxious attachments in their children.

Those with an avoidant attachment style will have a positive image of themselves but a negative one of others. They will be overly independent and uncomfortable with closeness.

The Stages of Attachment Development

Bowlby has identified four stages in the development of attachments. They are pre-attachment, attachment in the making, clear-cut attachment, and goal corrected.

Pre-Attachment

The pre-attachment stage occurs between birth and two months.

During this early stage, the infant shows interest and is responsive to interactions with anyone they encounter. They have a general attachment in that they have not yet developed an attachment to any single individual. For this reason, they are not stressed if a loving and responsive caregiver takes over for the primary caregiver. What is important to the infant is that the person can comfort them.

Attachment-in-the-Making

This second stage occurs between two and six months. The infant begins to develop a preference for an individual caregiver. They express their attachment through smiling and vocalizing. This is also the stage when the infant shows anxiety when they encounter someone they do not know. For the infant, this is a reaction to potential danger.

At this stage of attachment development, the baby does not only develop an attachment with its primary care giver but with others as well. This is also the stage when babies become more mobile and start to explore. They start crawling to investigate their world while keeping an eye on the primary caregiver. The presence of the primary caregiver gives the baby the confidence to explore.

Clear—Cut Attachment

Occurring between six months and two years, this is the stage where the child develops a strong attachment to their primary caregiver. They show signs of distress if separated from the primary caregiver for more than a brief period of time. In cases of prolonged separation, children can develop major trauma should they not be able to form a new attachment.

At this stage, the child's attachment with others is deeply ingrained. The child has created IWMs of its relationships. As the child ages, this internal model becomes more and more difficult to change.

As our IWMs operate subconsciously, they become our version of reality. We may not even be aware that our relationship issues are due to our attachment styles, because we have lived by our IWMs for most of our lives. If we become aware of how these models affect us, it takes a patient but determined effort to overcome their influence.

Goal-Corrected Partnership

This fourth stage occurs from age three to adolescence. This is the stage where there is greater tolerance for not having to be with the primary caregiver, given that the child knows where their caregiver is and their availability to them. It is also the stage when children learn that others are separate individuals with their own personalities, thoughts, and desires.

At this phase, there is a transformation in the child's attachment relationships. The child's understanding of relationships moves from focusing on getting its needs met to one where reciprocal relationship are formed. This is the stage where the child uses language to express their needs and is aware of space and time. At this stage, the child can benefit by regularly engaging with others, as in the case of pre-school.

How children respond in stage four will be shaped by the quality of attachments they form in the earlier stages.

What goes into a Child's Attachment?

Two factors determine how a child's attachments will develop: quality and critical period.

Quality

Research shows a child's primary attachment figure is not based on how much time a person spends with the child, but rather the quality of the time that the person provides them. The primary attachment is the strongest form of connection for the child. The child also forms additional attachments with those other than the primary attachment figures.

These additional attachments, also known as subsidiary attachments, vary in their level of intensity. A baby can form stronger attachments with people other than the primary caregiver if others provide a greater quality experience than the primary caregiver.

Critical Period

The critical period, also known as the sensitive period or the attachment in the making stage, is the period when a child's early attachments are formed. During this time, the brain's plasticity is receptive to the influence of the attachment experience. When this period passes, the child's attachment pattern becomes deeply ingrained and difficult to change.

Theories on Attachment Formation

This chapter covered the importance of forming attachments, the stages of attachment forming, and the factors that influence the creation of attachments. But how are attachments formed? There are two theories regarding this: learning theory and evolutionary.

Learning Theory

Under the learning theory, all of our behaviors are learned as opposed to being innate or instinctual. In other words, the child is born as a blank slate. The child learns different behaviors through conditioning. One form of conditioning has to do with association.

Because the mother is present when the baby gets fed, the baby learns to associate the mother with food. Conditioning can also be involved in behavior. The child learns that by engaging in a specific behavior, the child gets rewarded. An example of this is when the baby smiles and the mother smiles back or kisses the baby.

Because the behavior led to a favorable outcome, the baby will repeat this behavior in the future. Conversely, if the baby engages in a specific behavior that leads to a negative outcome, it will avoid repeating that behavior in the future.

Evolutionary Theory

While learning theory is based on the idea that our attachments to others come about through the process of learning, the evolutionary theory concludes that our need for attachment is hardwired within us from birth. Both Bowlby and Harlow believed that we are born preprogrammed to form attachments to others for the purpose of survival.

Under this theory, infants are born with the means to connect with others. These means come in the form of smiling, crying, and other behaviors that elicit adult nurturing responses. Bowlby believed that the infant forms just one attachment initially and that attachment is with the primary caregiver. It is this attachment that allows the child to explore their world.

This theory suggests that attachments must be formed within the first five years. If an attachment is not made within this period, the child will develop irreversible consequences to its development, such as increased aggression and reduced intelligence. In the next chapter, we look at how attachment styles affect relationships.

CHAPTER 2

How Attachment Styles Affect Relationships

Have you ever reached the point where you gave up on finding that special person who you dreamed of having a relationship with? Perhaps you found yourself falling into a pattern of having relationships with partners who were emotionally exhausting or emotionally unavailable. You may have started to doubt yourself and feel something was wrong with you.

Some researchers believe that our bonding experience with our first relationships, which were with our caregivers, may influence how we relate to intimacy later in life. The four attachment styles can provide us with insight into not only the behavior of our partners but also our own. With this understanding, we can better understand our needs and how to handle the challenges we experience.

Our attachment style influences who we pick as partners and how the relationship will progress. The reason is that our intimate relationships can trigger the attachment styles we adopted as children. In fact, we unconsciously select partners that conform to our attachment styles. We may continue to operate from our attachment styles even though they cause us unhappiness. The following are some examples of relationship patterns that come from an anxious attachment style:

- A tendency to be clingy with one's partner.

- Becoming easily jealous.

- Being more invested in the relationship than one's partner.

- The desire to be with one's partner but backing off when emotional closeness arises.

A person who developed an anxious attachment in childhood is likely to select a partner with an attachment style that mirrors their caregiver's. At an unconscious level, we may select partners that will respond to us as our caregivers did. How we behave in intimate relationships can be governed by our expectations originating from our childhood experiences. In other words, our attachment style can cause us to behave toward our partners in the same way we behaved toward our caregivers as children. The following are ways that our attachment styles impact our adult relationships:

Secure Attachment Style

Those with a secure attachment style develop meaningful relationships where they feel stable and safe. They develop meaningful relationships where they thrive. Further, they establish reasonable boundaries where they thrive and are not afraid to be alone.

It is not that those with a secure attachment style never experience insecurity or that they do not experience relationship problems. The difference is that they feel confident enough to own up to their mistakes and take responsible action to improve things.

Additionally, those with a secure attachment style turn to their partners when they need help or support. The following are characteristics of a relationship when a secure attachment style is involved:

- You recognize your self-worth and can be yourself. Also, you express your needs, feelings, and hopes freely.

- You can enjoy yourself when you are with people other than your partner and are comfortable when you are not with them.

- Not only are you comfortable going to your partner for support, but you are also comfortable with them coming to you when they need to.

- You can manage your emotions and work with your partner to resolve conflict healthily.

- You are resilient enough to bounce back when faced with relationship disappointments or setbacks.

Children with a secure attachment toward their caregivers see them as a source of comfort and security. This security allows them to explore the world around them. In a romantic relationship, this same attachment leads to a similar connection with their intimate partner. This security provides the freedom for partners to live their lives as individuals and as a couple.

Anxious Attachment Style

Someone with an anxious attachment style may be clingy in their relationships and have a continuous need for attention and love. They may be embarrassed by this need. Additionally, they may be emotionally drained by their ongoing concern about whether their partner truly loves them. Other characteristics of the anxious attachment style include:

- You genuinely desire closeness and intimacy with your partner, but you are held back because you do not feel you can trust or rely on them.

- Your intimate relationship consumes your life; your partner is your primary focus.

- You lack boundaries for yourself and frequently violate the boundaries of your partner. Your partner's desire for space threatens you. Situations like this may cause you to experience fear, panic, or anger. These feelings may lead you to believe that your partner is no longer interested in you.

- Your self-esteem is determined by how you feel your partner is treating you. Also, you jump to conclusions and overreact when you perceive a threat to the relationship.

- When you are not with your partner, you become anxious. You may become controlling or make them feel guilty to keep them close.

- You require continuous attention and reassurance from your partner.

- You have difficulty maintaining intimate relationships.

For those with this attachment style, their relationships follow a predictable pattern. The beginning of the relationship is marked by excitement and anticipation of what the relationship could become. There is that first kiss and the anticipation for when they can be with the other person. This relationship stage has an addictive quality, as there is a dopamine release.

At some point in the relationship, it is common for things to level out. The anxious attachment style partner's excitement and anticipation turn into anxiousness or concern. This person will start wondering if their partner is losing interest in them. This sense of doubt puts their partner in a losing position.

Even if their partner gives this person their attention and reassurance, the person with the anxious style attachment will never be satisfied as their hunger is like a bottomless pit. They will continue to believe that their partner is losing interest in them.

This person will engage in thoughts such as:

- Why does my partner not desire me the way that I desire them?

- Why have they not called me? I have not heard from them all day.

- I need to be more attentive to them, and then they will desire me more.

Unlike the authentic bond that secure attached couples enjoy, those with an anxious attachment style strive to fulfill a bond that is built on a fantasy. Rather than experiencing genuine love, their bond is based on an emotional hunger. They look for a partner to rescue or make them feel complete. This approach normally backfires as it causes their partner to back away.

Avoidant Attachment Style

Those with an avoidant attachment style are uncomfortable with emotional intimacy. For these individuals, freedom and independence are very important to them. They feel threatened by intimacy and closeness within a relationship. The following are examples of how an avoidant attachment style affects a romantic relationship:

- A person with this attachment style will be very independent and not feel that they need others.

- They will pull away when their partner tries to get close emotionally.

- If this is your style, you will be uncomfortable expressing your emotions. Your partner may claim that you are being distant. You may counter by accusing them of being needy.

- Those with this attachment style will dismiss their partner's feelings. They also may keep secrets from their partner and have affairs. Having affairs is a way for them to reclaim their sense of freedom.

- They are more comfortable with temporary or casual relationships than intimate and long-term ones. If they seek a relationship, they will be attracted to someone who is also independent. By doing so, they can remain emotionally distant.

- Intellectually, those with an avoidant attachment believe they do not need intimacy. In their hearts, however, they do desire a close and meaningful relationship. They resist this desire because they have a deep fear of intimacy.

Those with this style of attachment focus on their own needs. They want to turn to their partner to meet their needs, but their fear of getting hurt severely handicaps them. They put themselves in a no-win situation and do not get their needs met.

Now that we have covered the main attachment styles and how they affect relationships, we will take a deep dive into the anxious attachment style, which begins in the next chapter.

CHAPTER 3

The Anxious Attachment Style

Before discussing the anxious attachment style, it is useful to consider the importance of attachments. The development of attachments is an evolutionary mechanism to increase the probability of the survival of vulnerable individuals, including children.

The attachment system evolved as a response to the fears or distress of the individual. It promotes survival by promoting proximity between the caregiver and the child. The proximity reduces stress and anxiety in the child and increases its probability of survival so that it can mature and reproduce.

The attachment mechanism remains activated when the child's sense of security is inadequate. As the child grows, it develops a mental record (IWM) of its ability to receive proximity and comfort from its caregiver. This mental record remains with the individual as they advance toward other relationships, including friends, parents, and romantic partners. The individual experiences these other relationships through the same mental record they had with their caregiver.

The mental record is comprised of two parts: a mental record of significant others and a record of one's self. The mental record of significant others contains information on how others responded to the individual when they were in distress. The mental record of one's self contains information on an individual's ability to attract proximity and comfort and one's worth as a partner in the relationship. The need for a sense of security is as real for us today as it was in primordial times.

It is common to experience periods of insecurity within a relationship, fearing that a loved one will leave us. However, this is taken to an extreme for those with an anxious attachment style. For these individuals, the feelings of insecurity and fear of loss are so strong that they take over the relationship.

Those with an anxious attachment style have developed a mental representation of relationships that makes them uncertain whether or not they can count on their partner. This doubt increases their distress and makes them feel even less safe.

As a result, those with an anxious attachment become hyper-vigilant and sensitive toward their partner's responses.

Those with an anxious attachment style have a deep need for acceptance and engage in people-pleasing behaviors. The real cost to those with this attachment style is when their people-pleasing behaviors prevent them from being able to value themselves or recognize their own needs.

All of this sustains or escalates their anxiousness and makes their relationships unsatisfying. Approximately 19% of the population has an anxious attachment style.

How Anxious Attachment Styles are Created

From the time we are infants, we learn that we can get our emotional and physical needs met by our caregivers. When our caregiver is responsive to our needs, we develop a secure attachment style.

The story changes for the child that perceives that it cannot depend on its caregiver to meet its needs. There are times when the caregiver may be loving and responsive. Other times, the caregiver's response may be unloving, or they may ignore the child. When this happens, the child cannot form a secure bond with their caregiver as they receive mixed signals. This unstable relationship creates an anxious attachment style for the child. As with all attachment styles, the anxious attachment style lays the foundation for how the child will experience relationships as it progresses into adulthood.

However, inconsistency by the caregiver is not the only way a child can develop an anxious attachment style. The anxious attachment style can be passed down from generation to generation. Some caregivers have deep emotional neediness. The caregiver depends on the child to fulfill their need for emotional and physical closeness.

These caregivers may act overly intrusive or protective in caring for the child. Their intention is to meet their own need for love, or to create the image that they are the "perfect parent." The caregiver might be unaware of their self-serving behavior if they have been raised the same way by their own parents. The caregiver is unknowingly passing their anxious attachment style on to their child.

An overprotective parent may appear to respond to their child's needs effectively. However, the problem is that the caregiver is responding to their own needs instead of the child's. As with the inconsistent caregiver, the needy caregiver is not meeting the child's needs. Instead, they may behave in a clinging manner toward their child to fill their own emotional void. Not focusing on the needs of the child creates a generational cycle of anxious attachment.

When a caregiver focuses on the child, the child feels safe and cared for. As early as infancy, the child is absorbing information about their experiences with their caregiver. When the child cannot experience the caregiver's attention and calmness, they are left feeling uncertain.

Regardless of the cause, the child internalizes this anxious attachment and brings it into their adult relationships. The cycle continues if they do not work on themselves and then choose to have children.

There are situations where a child can develop an anxious attachment from having a caregiver who has an avoidant attachment style. Because the avoidant parent cannot meet the child's emotional needs, the child grows up and looks to their adult romantic relationships for what they did not get during childhood. In this case, this person unconsciously tries to bring healing to their deprived inner child. However, this never works.

As adults enter a romantic relationship, they will carry the same uncertainty about their partner as they did with their caregiver. In other words, they will doubt their partner will be there for them.

Which Children Are at the Greatest Risk?

The following are the childhood experiences that may increase the probability of developing an anxious attachment style:

- Being separated from the parent or caregiver at an early age.

- Physical or sexual abuse.

- Incidents of mistreatment or neglect.

- Having a caregiver responds with annoyance or ridicule when the child is in distress.

Signs of Anxious Attachment

Style in Children

The following are signs that a child may have an anxious attachment style:

- They become very distressed when they are separated from their parents.

- When they are upset, they are inconsolable. They will not respond to attempts to comfort them.

- They are clingy toward their caregivers.

- They are fearful of strangers.

- They have difficulty forming relationships with other children.

- There is a hesitation to explore their environment.

- Their general appearance is that of being anxious.

- It is difficult for them to regulate or control their negative emotions.

- They behave aggressively.

Signs of Anxious Attachment Style in Adults

The following signs in adults may be due to an anxious attachment style:

- They have low self-esteem and see others as being better than them.

- They are attuned to the needs of their partner but neglect their own.

- If their partner does not meet their needs, they blame themselves and believe they are not worthy of love.

- They need continuous reassurance that they are loved and that they are good enough.

- They can be extremely suspicious or jealous of their partner.

- Their fear of abandonment can lead them to become preoccupied with their relationship.

- They are uncomfortable being alone.

- Low self-esteem.

- The constant need for intimacy and closeness.

- Fear of being abandoned.

- They are overly dependent on their relationship.

- They are people-pleasers, and they constantly need approval.

- It is difficult for them to trust their partner. This lack of trust comes from being unable to depend on their caregiver as a child.

- Being very sensitive toward their partner's moods and actions.

- They fixate or overanalyze minor situations.

- They experience a pattern of not experiencing love in their relationships.

- They are overly attentive to their partner's needs with the motive of wanting their partner to need them.

- They take responsibility for most of the blame and guilt that exist in the relationship.

The following are examples of anxious attachment style behaviors:

- You text or call your partner repeatedly until you receive a response from them.

- You frequently check their social media accounts.

- You feel suspicious when there is calm in the relationship.

- You participate in whatever activities your friends want, even when you would rather be doing something else.

- You overextend yourself at work by taking on extra projects to please your co-workers.

- You have difficulty saying "no," even when you really want to.

- You continually ask your partner if they find you attractive.

- You will do anything to avoid ending a relationship, even when you know that the relationship is not healthy for you.

Adults with an anxious attachment style believe they have to earn their partners' love and approval, instead of believing they deserve to be loved. As we will see later, this dynamic often causes those with an anxious attachment style to be attracted to those with an avoidant attachment style.

In such relationships, the anxious attached partner has to work for their partner's attention. This kind of relationship feels natural to them. Conversely, they would find it boring to be with a partner who freely gives love and attention.

In the next chapter, we will take a deeper look into how the anxious attachment style impacts relationships.

CHAPTER 4

The Anxious Attachment Style in Relationships

Being in a relationship with someone with an anxious attachment style is like being on an emotional roller coaster. In such relationships, things can be intense and stressful for both partners. The partner with the anxious attachment style can become like a bottomless pit in their need for validation from their partner. Regardless of how often they receive validation from their partner, the partner with this attachment type will continue to anticipate being abandoned.

The mindset that comes with this attachment style leads to a self-fulfilling prophecy. At the subconscious level, such individuals expect to be rejected and will be attracted to individuals who are not emotionally available for a healthy relationship. When this happens, the anxious styled partner will make an extra effort to persuade their partner to stay in the relationship. What often occurs is that the other partner will eventually take advantage of them by treating them badly. This dynamic becomes a vicious cycle.

Even if the partner does not take advantage of the anxious styled individual, they will experience much pressure due to their partner's neediness and are likely to distance themselves from them. For the anxious styled partner, healing comes when they learn to be able to trust that their partner loves and cares about them. Until then, their continuous doubt will most likely lead to a relationship decline.

The following are some characteristics of such relationships:

Clinginess

In the relationship, the person with the anxious attachment style may become fixated on their partner. They are likely to want to rush into the relationship and want their partner to commit to them. These individuals often fall in love quickly and become obsessed with their partners. Additionally, they may look to their partner to fulfill all of their desires, which creates anxiety for both partners.

Long-distance relationships with anxious attachment types are more difficult than with non-attached partners, because it creates great anxiety for them.

Rejection Fears

Those with an anxious attachment continuously fear their partners breaking off the relationship, or not being there for them in their times of need. They are hyper-vigilant and have the mindset that their partner will leave them. Because of this, they are triggered by any sign of disappointment or disagreement with their partner. This ongoing fear is a product of their low self-esteem.

They will blame themselves if their partner does not respond to their needs or rejects them for any reason. Their partner's response will reinforce their belief that they are not worthy of being loved.

Constant Need for Reassurance

It is both normal and healthy to seek reassurance from one's partner.

The challenge with anxiously attached individuals is that they are persistent in their need for reassurance. This persistent need can be emotionally draining for their partner as they must continuously prove their love to them.

Emotional Instability

As mentioned earlier, relationships with those who have an anxious attachment style can feel like an emotional rollercoaster. Partners never know what to expect from the anxiously attached person. They may be high or low, filling the relationship with stress and anxiety.

Further, the relationship quality is usually low for both partners. The partner becomes frustrated with the other person's constant need for reassurance, while the person with an anxious attachment will become anxious because of their partner's frustration.

Feelings of Being Unappreciated

Those with an anxious attachment style often feel unappreciated as they do not feel they are getting the love and attention they deserve. The challenge is that their continuous need for reassurance makes it unrealistic for their partner to give them the appreciation that they desire.

It is common for this attachment style to feel unappreciated, which causes them to worry about their place in the relationship. They can become consumed with the thought that their partner does not love them as much as they love their partner. Those with an anxious attachment style may be clinging to a fantasy of how the relationship should be, and they evaluate the relationship based on that fantasy.

They have trouble understanding that relationships are dynamic and that the way the relationship started (the honeymoon state) cannot be expected to last. When the partner no longer treats them as they did at the beginning of the relationship, the anxious attached will become suspicious of their partner. They will likely accuse their partner of not appreciating them or believe they are unworthy of love.

What further makes dealing with anxious attachment partners challenging is that they avoid expressing their feelings, as they fear showing vulnerability. Because they do not express their feelings, they do not get their needs met. In place of expressing their feelings, they act defensively or provocatively.

Those with an anxious attachment style normally have a positive view of others but a negative one of themselves. They tend to overly idealize their romantic relationships, on which they build their self-esteem.

The Dance of Opposites

Those with an anxious attachment style are frequently attracted to people with an avoidant attachment style. As a reminder, those with an avoidant attachment style avoid intimacy.

Why would someone who craves intimacy be attracted to someone who avoids it? The answer is the person who has the anxious attachment has been programmed by their past to expect their partner will not give them the attention they desire. The one with the avoidant attachment style fits the mental model that the anxiously attached person developed with their caregiver.

All couples engage in a psychological dance, where they balance their needs for intimacy. In this dance, one partner moves forward while the other steps back. In other words, one partner wants to move toward emotional intimacy while the other wants to step away from it. The partners do not do this consciously, and they are continuously switching roles.

In a normal relationship, this dance functions to maintain a balance in emotional intimacy. At some point, the partner who advances will retreat, while the partner who retreats will advance.

This dance reflects a dilemma that we all face. We have a conflicting need for both intimacy and autonomy. We also have a fear of being too close and a fear of being abandoned. This is the dilemma that is posed by intimacy.

When an anxious attachment partner enters a relationship with an avoidant style partner, the partners never change roles. The anxious partner is always pursuing, and the avoidant partner is always backing away. One partner is always seeking intimacy, and the other always avoids it.

Those with the anxious attachment style are subconsciously drawn to those who are emotionally unavailable. The person with the anxious attachment will work hard to get their avoidant attached partner to stay with them. However, the avoidant style partner is programmed to avoid intimacy. The avoidant attached partner's behavior validates the fears of the anxiously attached partner that they are unlovable. The dynamics of the relationship create a vicious cycle.

The Origins of Anxious and Avoidant Dance

This dance between anxious and avoidant partners highlights how we can be impacted by our relationship as children with our caregivers. The anxious attachment style is often caused by an emotionally unavailable parent or caregiver. Babies and young children depend on their caregivers to have empathy for them. They need that person to be responsive to their needs and emotions. Through this responsiveness, babies develop a sense of self and wholeness.

For the development of that sense of wholeness to take place, children depend on validation from their caregivers. Unfortunately, that validation may not occur if the caregiver is emotionally unavailable, suffering from illness, or neglects the child for other reasons. If the caregiver lacks self-esteem, is depressed, or is ill, they may lack healthy boundaries between them and the child.

Instead of responding to the child's needs, they will view the child as an extension of themselves. They will view the child as a way to meet their own feelings and needs. The caregiver is unable to view the child as a separate self. As a result, there is a violation of the child's boundaries. The child's thoughts and feelings are disrespected.

As a result, the child is not given a chance to develop a healthy sense of self. Instead, the child learns they must meet the caregiver's needs to gain love and approval. Furthermore, they learn to focus on the caregiver's expectations and responses. The result is that the child develops a sense of shame and codependency. As the child develops, they may lose touch with their thoughts, feelings, and needs.

When the child reaches adulthood, the experience of being separated from an intimate partner awakens those pains and fears from early on. The anxious partner will feel abandoned if the avoidant partner does not meet their needs and feelings. In this case, both partners find themselves in a codependent relationship where neither is a separate and whole person. As a result, there is no emotional intimacy. In its place is the fear of dissolution and subsequent nonexistence.

Relationships: The Mirrors to Our Concealments

Many do not realize that there is a reason why we are drawn to certain people. The people with whom we enter a relationship provide a mirror to our hidden worlds. We try to repress or disown some aspects of ourselves, which we often do unconsciously.

We invite those who are our opposite into our lives. Unconsciously, we do so in the hopes that they will make us feel whole. The individual who has an anxious attachment style is fearful of abandonment. However, they also have a fear of intimacy. This is why those with an anxious attachment style find themselves drawn to those with an avoidant attachment style. The individual with the anxious attachment style is looking to the avoidant partner to create the space needed for them to experience independence and autonomy.

Similarly, the avoidant partner fears becoming trapped. They avoid emotional closeness as that would make them vulnerable. For this reason, they rely on their anxious partner to meet their intimacy needs.

The internal dialogue of the avoidant attachment style goes something like this:

"My partner is too needy, dependent, or emotional."

Simultaneously, they are also asking themselves:

"Am I capable of love, or am I too selfish? It seems that whatever I give it is never enough."

In the case of the anxious partner, they are telling themselves:

"My partner always has to have their way. They are emotionally withdrawn, inconsiderate, and selfish."

Simultaneously, they are asking themselves:

"Is there something wrong with me? Is it that I am not pretty, smart, or successful enough?"

Both partners blame each other and themselves. The anxious partner feels resentful that they are not getting their needs met, while the avoidant partner feels guilty that they are not meeting their partner's needs. However, something even deeper is happening in the minds of this couple.

The anxious partner judges the part of themselves that is independent or selfish, while the avoidant partner judges the part of themselves that is vulnerable, needy, and dependent.

However, both partners are projecting the part of themselves that they cannot accept onto their partner.

In such a relationship, the avoidant partner will push away the anxious partner. In response, the anxious partner will become more determined to connect with the avoidant partner. They may be relentless in their attempts to be with them.

The anxious partner's behavior only emboldens the avoidant partner with the confidence that they can do whatever they want, and the anxious partner will be there waiting for them. This is the playbook by which both partners use to experience intimacy. Both partners need to accept and embrace all aspects of themselves to heal.

The Anxious Attachment Style in the WorkPlace

How attachment styles play out in the workplace has not received much attention from researchers; however, this is changing. There has been more research in this area within the last five years than in the previous 25 years combined. One study involved the social dynamics of attachment theory in the workplace. They studied how attachment style dynamics affected workers and those in leadership positions. Their findings are as follows:

Anxious Attachment Style in Workers

Workers with anxious attachment styles can create conflict in the workplace due to their constant need for approval. Those with this attachment style tend to be highly insecure and have self-doubt, leading to the need for continuous approval from their co-workers.

Because they want to please everyone, they conform to "group think." They also avoid confrontation and are constantly looking to be praised for their work. The challenge in the workplace is that these things become their priority. The result is that the unrealistic expectations and demands that they have for themselves can create an uncomfortable work environment.

Further, those with this attachment style do not function well when working alone. When they are part of a team, they may lean on others for help completing their work. Because of their constant need for approval, they tend to be more sensitive toward constructive feedback, more likely to feel unappreciated, and more likely to be dissatisfied with their jobs. The result of all this is a higher frequency of burnout.

Although the anxious attachment style can pose challenges to the workplace, it also has positive qualities. Those with this attachment style quickly detect workplace threats or risks because of their hyper-vigilance. Additionally, they are very self-reflective and are aware of the areas in which they fall short. This quality, along with their desire to please others, means that they are continuously working on improving themselves.

Finally, this is one attachment style you do not have to worry about being a troublemaker. Because of their desire to belong, they will follow workplace norms. In the next chapter, we will discuss ways to cope with an anxious attachment style.

CHAPTER 5

How to Cope with Your Anxious Attachment Style

The anxious attachment style is not a form of mental illness. It is formed in childhood when our caregivers do not meet our emotional needs. As with the other attachment styles, the anxious attachment style was adopted to cope with this reality. The challenge is that these adaptations no longer support us as we age.

Changing one's attachment style is very difficult because it becomes part of one's personality. Because of this, changing one's attachment style requires constant vigilance. Instead of trying to change one's attachment style, it is more practical to learn how to cope with it and develop a more secure attachment style.

Each of us has the potential to create change in our lives, regardless of age. Anxious attachment styles are the result of our deep-seated beliefs. However, we can change them. Creating a change in our beliefs requires that we challenge them. To do so, however, requires support, practice, and patience. This is because our self-talk, our harshest critic, will hinder our attempts to change.

This voice was developed from our childhood experience and will do its best to keep us from experiencing our emotions. It is the discomfort of these emotions that the insecure attachment styles are designed to save us from.

Fortunately, recognizing one's insecure attachment style is half the battle in creating change. There can be no healing without self-awareness. Understanding one's attachment style lets one know what one must work on. Developing a more secure attachment style is definitely possible regardless of one's insecure attachment style.

Awareness is the organizing principle behind all change, including changes in attachment styles. True healing comes from learning to make sense of how one interacts with others, especially one's partners. By recognizing one's behavioral patterns in relationships, and becoming mindful of them, creating empowering change becomes that much easier. It is for this reason that self-reflection is so important.

Bringing Awareness to Anxious Attachment

Those with an anxious attachment style are normally reactive to what they perceive as a negative situation. In other words, they are on autopilot. They automatically respond to the situation without thinking about it. When we become more aware of how we respond, we can think of more empowering ways to respond.

Coping Strategies for the Anxious Attachment Style

If you have an anxious attachment style, you can develop a more secure attachment pattern by understanding your coping strategies and learning how to respond in more empowering ways. You can begin by asking yourself the following questions:

How do I create closeness in my relationship? Examples of answers to this question include:

- I do not disagree with my partner.

- I act seductively.

- I become my partner's caretaker.

- I engage in people-pleasing behavior.

In my efforts to build closeness, what do I give up? Examples of answers to this question include:

- I give up my autonomy.

- I give up my hobbies and interests.

- I give up my friendships.

- I give up my right to disagree.

When you engage in these behaviors without being aware of them, you aren't doing so by choice, but due to your unconscious thinking patterns. Because of this, you are unable to communicate your needs effectively. Rather, you are unconsciously trying to manipulate your partner. If your partner has an avoidant attachment style, they are doing the same thing to you.

Overcoming the anxious attachment styles involves learning new ways of thinking that support our happiness and being able to connect with others. Though this may sound simple, making such a change takes patience, determination, and persistence. As healthier ways of viewing ourselves and others sink in, the corresponding behaviors and emotions will follow.

Making such a change can be difficult and scary because it requires learning to trust oneself and others, both of which go against the way insecure attachment styles are programmed. However, it can be done! A good place to start is learning about your triggers.

Anxious Attachment Style Triggers

The signs of the anxious attachment style do not appear all the time. Rather, they are triggered by the behaviors of their partners. The following are examples of triggers that can activate the anxious attachment style:

- Arguments

- Inconsistent behavior by a partner.

- The partner arrives home later than expected.

- When the partner seems distracted or distant.

- The partner forgets an important occasion, like an anniversary or birthday.

- Not receiving a call or message from a partner when it was expected.

- The partner fails to notice something important to the individual.

- Their partner does not appear to be paying attention to them because they are involved in a project or activity.

- A breach of trust by the partner.

When this attachment style is triggered, the individual experiences increased self-doubt and insecurity. The following are examples of what the anxiously attached individual may think when hearing the following from their partners:

Partner: "I need some time to be with myself."

Anxious Attached: What did I do wrong? Or, how can I fix the situation?

Partner: "Sorry I did not call you earlier; I was talking to some people I know."

Anxious Attached: Who was he talking to? Why are they more important than me?

Partner: "I need to reschedule our plans. I have to get caught up in my work."

Anxious Attached: My partner is cheating on me. I will not let them get away with this!

Modern Technology as a Trigger

Our modern technology has enormous benefits for us in terms of accessing information and communicating with each other. However, for those of us with an anxious attachment style, technology can also heighten our insecurity. Let's use texting as an example. Texting can compound the feeling of insecurity that people with anxious attachment experience. The following are examples:

- The anxious partner starts to panic when they do not receive a text from their partner to confirm upcoming plans.

- The anxious partner texts someone they are interested in, but that person does not reply.

- The anxious partner receives a reply from their person of interest and scrutinizes it if it does not meet their expectations.

Triggered Behaviors

When we give in to our anxious attachment style, we give into the emotions that come up when we are triggered. The following are examples of triggered behavior:

- Making repeated attempts to connect or reconnect with a partner.

- Withdrawing

- Being hostile

- Keeping score

- Making threats of leaving

- Manipulating others

- Attempting to make your partner jealous.

How to Handle Triggers in Yourself

You can learn to overcome your triggers if you have an anxious attachment style. The following are some suggestions:

Remember to Breathe

One of the most important things you can do is remember to breathe. Focusing on your breathing will ground you in your body and keep you from getting caught up in your emotions.

When you feel triggered, pause and focus on your breath. Notice the sensations that you experience in your body. If you feel stress in your body, do not try to change it. Instead, accept that it exists and focus on your breath and bodily sensations.

Interrupt Your Thoughts

If you feel triggered, interrupt your thought pattern by changing your thinking to something positive. An example of interrupting your thoughts is to think about planning something that you would like to do, such as planning a vacation. Doing this will keep you from running your habitual thought patterns. If you do not engage in your usual thinking, you will not become emotionally excited as easily. Naturally, this method takes consistent practice for it to become effective.

Place Yourself Behind the Wheel

Another method for overcoming your triggers is to place yourself in the driver's seat. Focus on the thought that you are the hero of your own story and are in charge of your happiness. You will gradually learn to be less reactive to your partner by putting yourself in control.

In using any of these suggestions, it is important to note that it takes consistent practice to make a difference. It is also important to remember that you are trying to change a behavior pattern that you have had since you were a child. For these reasons, you are advised to be patient and gracious with yourself and your partner as you learn to change your reactions when triggered.

Awareness of Your Physiology

Triggering the anxious attachment style results in the flight, fight, or freeze response. The flight or fight response is well known. In the face of danger, animals will either flee or defend themselves. The freeze response is something that occurs in this attachment style. The response is one of confusion. The person is unable to think clearly. When this happens, the person will go by their first impulse.

You can remove yourself from the freeze response by taking a moment to breathe. Focus on the sensations of your breath as you breathe. You may also want to place your hands on your abdomen to connect with its movements as it rises and falls.

By doing this, you are redirecting your attention from your thinking and signaling to your brain that you are safe. Also, there are numerous grounding activities that you can do when you feel anxious. Consider exercising, meditating, doing yoga, taking a walk-in nature, or getting a massage.

Learn to Self-Soothe

An important part of moving beyond your anxious attachment style is learning to self-soothe, which is especially important when coping with jealousy. Jealousy is a hallmark of the anxious attachment style. In fact, those with an anxious attachment style will often feel that their feelings are being reciprocated when their partner experiences jealousy.

For anxiously attached partners, jealousy can make them feel closer to their partners. Further, the feeling of jealousy makes them feel more alive. The anxious partner may feel more connected to their partner when they experience jealousy, taking it as a sign that their partner cares about them.

Naturally, this kind of mindset will not lead you to a more secure relationship style. It is important that you deal with your feelings of jealousy; an effective way of doing so is through self-soothing.

Dealing with jealousy through self-soothing starts with understanding that jealousy is usually a coping strategy used when anticipating loss. This fear of loss predates your adult relationships, beginning with your relationship with your primary caregiver. By doing inner child work, you can uncover the original source of your fears and become less reactive toward them.

The process's next step is to understand that jealousy can be used to serve you in your relationships. You allow your partner to experience your vulnerability by becoming honest with your feelings. What can come from this is a deeper connection between you and your partner. Your partner then has the opportunity to meet your needs.

Additionally, getting to know your jealousy can help you gain a deeper understanding of what you need to strengthen your self-esteem. This is because feelings of inadequacy, shame, disrespect, or failure are often the products of jealousy.

By mindfully confronting these products of jealousy, you can experience a broader range of emotions that elevate rather than disempower. The emotion of jealousy is a message that we need to tend to our own needs.

Nurture Your Inner Child

If you have an anxious attachment style, you likely developed it when you were a child. So bringing healing to that child is a great place to start. The term "inner child," refers to the emotional energy created when you were a child but still holds on to you today.

This emotional energy contains the memories of your interactions with your caregiver and the emotional pains you associate with them. So, the inner child is a metaphor, and it continues to influence you by causing you to feel and react today just as you did when you were a child.

Healing your inner child will require you to look within yourself and acknowledge the emotional pain that you experienced. When your emotional pain is recognized, you can then reparent your inner child by providing for its needs.

When working on your inner child, you will face resistance, so gaining your inner child's trust may take time. As you gain your inner child's trust, you can get in touch with what it is feeling.

Gaining your inner child's trust requires consistency on your part. You need to align what you say with what you do. In other words, your behavior needs to be more congruent with how you feel. To do this, it is important that you develop the attitude that you are deserving of what you need and to feel what you feel. This requires you not to allow anyone to keep you from being true to your inner child.

When you claim responsibility for your inner child, you can then commit to loving it. You need to treat your inner child the same way a loving mother treats her infant. You are committed to meeting all of its needs. When doing inner child work, we learn to experience a deep love that is both receiving and giving.

Having learned to care for your inner child, you will need to extend that into your relationship with your partner. This means you must prioritize your needs to balance them with your partner's needs. Further, you will need to learn to stop searching for validation through your partner. You need to learn that the only validation that you need is your own.

Bring Evidence to Faulty Thinking

When experiencing negative thought patterns, it is important to evaluate their truthfulness rather than just blindly accepting them as being accurate. When you experience a negative thought, challenge it.

Look for any evidence that may disprove the thought. For example, you may think that people cannot be trusted. You can challenge that thought by looking back to see if you ever had an encounter with someone who did not betray your trust. You can also explore other possible explanations for your thinking. You may believe someone violated your trust, but is it possible there is another explanation? Could it be that instead of intentionally violating your trust, they made a mistake or were unaware of what they were doing?

By creating a sense of doubt in our negative thinking, we weaken it and provide the opportunity for us to engage in less "black and white" thinking.

Express Yourself

Instead of allowing yourself to be consumed by your thoughts, express your feelings safely and enjoyably. The feelings you experience when anxious can be rendered harmless if you externalize them instead of bottling them up within you.

Find a way to express your feelings through creative means such as art, music, or dance. You can also record them in a journal. Another approach is to journal from the perspective of your inner child. Discover why your inner child is feeling the way they do.

Rehearse Your Script

If you anticipate having an important conversation, prepare for it in advance. Just as an actor practices their lines, you can practice the message you want to give. Make your message honest, kind, and clear so that you do not come across as being controlling or needy.

Get To Know the Secure Attachment Style

Start forming relationships with people who have a secure attachment style. By doing so, you will be able to learn what a secure and stable relationship is like. By doing so, you may be able to interrupt your pattern of going after individuals who have an avoidant attachment style.

Practice Being Vulnerable

To develop a more secure type of attachment, try focusing on being more vulnerable while simultaneously creating emotional safety for yourself. One example is to step out of your comfort zone by clearly expressing how you feel about a situation.

Explicitly state what you want and what you do not want. Learn to clearly express to others your feelings, needs, and desires, even if you are concerned about their reaction.

Associating with people who have a secure attachment style will help you learn how to handle yourself in interpersonal situations where you are assertive but emotionally safe.

Increase Your Emotional Intelligence

Also called emotional quotient (EQ), emotional intelligence is the ability to understand, employ, and manage one's emotions in a way that benefits the relationship. The relationship benefits through greater empathy for one's partner, effective communication, and healthy conflict resolution.

By increasing your emotional intelligence, you can also express your needs more effectively to your partner and improve your understanding of how your partner feels.

Deal with Childhood Trauma

As mentioned earlier, childhood trauma can lead to an insecure attachment style by disrupting the attachment process. Childhood trauma can include any situation that threatens your sense of security as a child. Such situations may include an unstable or unsafe home environment, separation from your primary caregiver, or experiencing abuse, neglect, or serious illness. When our childhood trauma is not addressed, the feelings of fear, insecurity, and helplessness may be carried over into adulthood.

Taking Time for Yourself

Each day, take time for self-care. It is important that you do this consistently. In other words, make it part of your daily routine. Doing this will help calm your anxiety. Take time to do those things that you enjoy and find relaxing.

Strengthen Your Nonverbal Communication

The source of our attachment styles was our nonverbal communication with our primary caregiver when we were very young. Just as nonverbal communication determines the success of our relationship with our primary caregiver, it also plays a big role in determining the success of our adult relationships.

Though we may not be aware of it, we continuously give nonverbal signals as we interact with others. These nonverbal signals include things like our posture and eye contact. These signals communicate how we feel about a situation.

We can strengthen our relationships with others by learning to interpret and communicate non-verbally. You can develop this skill by learning to be present in the moment, managing stress, and developing greater emotional awareness. All of these things can be developed through the practice of mindfulness.

Practice Mindfulness

One of the challenges that many of us experience is that we overanalyze things and often do so from a negative perspective. This is especially true for those with an anxious attachment style. By practicing mindfulness, you can learn to focus on the present moment and manage any uncomfortable emotions in a way that empowers you.

Being present will make you feel more confident when interacting with others and develop greater confidence in the relationship. There are different ways to practice mindfulness, some include:

- Meditation

- Tai chi

- Yoga

- Walking meditation

- Gardening

Therapy

Getting therapy is very helpful for learning how to cope with anxious attachment styles. It will allow you to be in a safe place to explore thoughts and feelings and learn new and empowering ways to engage with others. Cognitive behavioral therapy (CBT) has been shown to be effective for identifying and changing negative thoughts and behavior patterns.

Another way to become more effective in interpersonal relationships and social interactions is through Interpersonal therapy (IPT). Psychodynamic psychotherapy is useful for recognizing how your emotions impact you at the subconscious level.

It is important to note that having an anxious attachment style does not mean something is wrong with you. Rather, you have learned a way to navigate relationships that most likely are not serving you in becoming fulfilled emotionally.

By understanding how your attachment style impacts you in your relationships, you can begin the process of learning how to manage it. Self-awareness and communication are key to managing thoughts and behaviors associated with this attachment style. This involves becoming aware of your attachment style and learning how to express what you are feeling.

Next time you feel triggered, examine how you are feeling at that moment and what you are thinking. Ask yourself what is the meaning that you are giving to the situation. If you do this, you will no longer be going on autopilot. You will be able to think of healthier ways to respond to the situation.

If you find this too difficult, you can remove yourself from the situation before responding. Find a place where you feel safe so that you can gather your thoughts before you go back to the situation.

In the next chapter, we will continue to explore ways to deal with this attachment style within the context of a relationship.

Chapter 6

The Anxious Attachment Style, Partners, and Dating

Whether you have an anxious attachment style or your partner does, there are things that you can do to improve the quality of the relationship. In this chapter, we will explore what you can do if you are dating, already in a relationship, and how you can support a partner who has an anxious attachment style. Though divided into sections, the suggestions listed are useful in all cases.

Dating and Anxious Attachment Style

You can take steps to prepare yourself better when dating or entering a relationship. As with the other suggestions in this chapter, these steps involve developing greater clarity about yourself and what you need. It all begins with your values.

Know Your Values and Needs

Take time to reflect on what you need from a relationship. If you have difficulty answering this question, it is important that you clarify this for yourself. If you are unclear about your needs, how will you or anyone else ever meet them?

You can begin identifying your needs by thinking about your past relationships and making a list of your criticisms. When you have completed your list, review the list from the perspective of your needs. For example, if one of your criticisms was that your previous partners did not make you feel appreciated, one of your needs may be feeling appreciated.

Besides looking at your unmet needs, look for patterns in your past relationships that did not support your happiness. Examples of this are long-distance relationships or relationships where your partners had difficulty expressing themselves. By doing this, you can distinguish between the patterns that worked for you and patterns that you did not need. You can then look for these patterns in the people you meet later on.

Break Your Pattern of Who You Date

As mentioned before, those with an anxious attachment style tend to gravitate toward individuals with an avoidant attachment style. Both the anxious attachment style and the avoidant attachment style are classified as insecure attachments. However, they have opposite needs.

The anxious attachment style craves reassurance and closeness, while the avoidant style seeks autonomy and space. The relationship dynamics are unlikely to change unless both partners desire to change. If you have an anxious attachment style, you would be better off seeking a relationship with someone with a secure attachment style.

Current Relationships and the Anxious Attachment Style

If you are already in a relationship, the following are suggestions for improving your relationship with your partner:

The Languages of Love

In his book, *the Five Love Languages,* Dr. Gary Chapman offers a useful tool for gaining clarification of your needs. Chapman discusses the five love languages. A love language is a specific way to express our love more effectively to others.

Each person has their own language of love. If you understand your partner's love language, they will more likely feel loved. The following are the five love languages:

Words of Affirmation: In this love language, you feel loved when you hear your partner compliment you or express their feelings for you.

Physical Touch: You feel loved when your partner touches you in this love language.

Quality Time: In this love language, you feel loved when your partner gives you their undivided attention or when they spend time with you.

Acts of Service: In this love language, you feel loved when your partner does something on your behalf.

Gifts: In this love language, you feel loved when your partner buys you or makes you something.

It is important to note that we may feel loved by all five of these languages; however, there is one language that is our main language. In other words, each person has one or more love languages that impact them most. If you know your love language, you can let your partner know it is one of your needs. Similarly, if you know your partner's love language, you can meet theirs.

How to Communicate Your Needs to Your Partner

You must communicate your needs to your partner early on in the relationship. It is also important that you communicate your needs clearly. The clearer you are in your communication, the more likely they will meet your needs. Additionally, communicating your needs early in the relationship increases your chances of determining if they are the right person for you.

If communication is important to you, let them know that and then see if they deliver on that.

If receiving compliments and reassurance is important to you, let them know that and see if they follow through. If it is important for you to know when you will see them next, tell them that and see if they will give you an answer. When you do this, you are letting them know what is important to you and seeing if they care enough to put in the effort to meet your needs.

Practice the Art of Detachment

The driving force of the anxious attachment style is to cling and hold on to their partner. What more powerful way could there be to deal with this attachment style than by doing the direct opposite? Why not try a Buddhist approach by following the principle of detachment?

If you have an anxious attachment style, you will likely spend a lot of time thinking about your relationship. However, much of what you think about is probably not in your control. These thoughts will likely trigger your attachment system, leading to fear and a need to cling to the relationship.

When practicing detachment, one does the opposite. Instead of being overwhelmed with fear and needing control, practicing detachment leads to being aware of the present moment without trying to control or resist anything. When practicing detachment, one shifts their attention from what cannot be controlled to what can be, which is ourselves. Great peace comes from experiencing the present moment with complete acceptance.

The principle of detachment is based on the idea that the only ones that we are responsible for are ourselves. We are unable to change anyone except ourselves. Detachment calls us to let life unfold without us trying to force or control the situation. You can begin to practice detachment by becoming aware of the emotions you experience when reacting to a situation.

The emotions you are experiencing are natural; they originate from the past but appear in the present. They do not come from what is happening outside yourself. Rather, they are of your creation and brought back to life when you are triggered.

Accept them as yours and take responsibility for them. You can take responsibility for them by deciding whether or not you will respond to them by taking action. Your emotions are neither good nor bad, for it is you who gives meaning to your emotions. With this in mind, the emotions that you experience can serve you. They are pointing out to you that there are unresolved issues from your past, and they are unresolved because you have not yet taken responsibility for them. To

take responsibility for your emotions is to accept them a:
them while realizing that they have no power over you, thou
feel that way.

The following are ways to remind yourself to stay detached from your emotions:

- How others treat me reflects their character, not mine.

- I have faith that everything will work out as it is intended to. Whatever happens, it is for the best.

- I do not have to deal with that today. I can wait until it is the right time for me.

- I can choose to let go and let things be.

- Whatever happens today was meant to happen. I will not struggle against the workings of the universe.

- If it is meant to happen to me, it will happen.

Turn to Your Creativity

Getting involved with your creativity is a great outlet for exercising your focus while calming your mind. If you feel anxious, turn to express yourself creatively by painting, drawing, coloring, singing, or writing.

Make Use of Your Support System

If you are becoming anxious, talk to a loved one or close friend. Sharing your feelings with others creates a win-win situation. You win by being able to unload what you are feeling, while they win by being allowed to express their compassion and support for you.

All these suggestions share in common that they provide an indirect means to getting your emotional needs taken care of. By doing so, you can get into a calmer state where you can more effectively communicate your needs to your partner. When we do not let others know what we need from them, we deny ourselves. Instead of reacting to your emotions, try to do the following:

1. Objectively describe to your partner what you experienced.

2. Explain to them how it made you feel.

3. When speaking to them, resort to "I" statements rather than "you."

4. While speaking to them, keep an even-toned voice. Avoid getting angry, yelling, or speaking over them.

The following is an example:

"I have not heard from you in a while, and I have a need to be honest with you. I feel anxious when we let days go by without speaking. Are you available to talk today? It would really mean a lot to me."

When phrased this way, you treat yourself and your partner with dignity.

What Would They Do?

It has been mentioned earlier that forming a relationship with someone who has a secure attachment style can help you develop a more secure attachment style. Next time you experience anxiety about your relationship, ask yourself this question, "What would someone with a secure attachment style do in this situation?" By asking this question, you are reframing the situation, allowing you to see it from a different perspective.

What You Can Do for an Anxiously Attached Partner

If you are in a relationship with an anxiously attached partner, the following are some suggestions on how you can support them:

Learn About Their Style

Learn about your partner's attachment style. The more you know about it, the better you will be equipped to understand them.

Don't Show Them…Tell Them

You will be more effective in showing gratitude to your partner if you tell them instead of showing them through your actions. The reason why is that those with this attachment style may not pick up on your intent unless you tell them. When expressing your appreciation to them, begin your statement with "Thank you for…" or "I appreciate that you…."

Knowing What to Say and Not to Say

To more effectively communicate with an anxious style partner, here are some examples of what not to say or do:

- "I am sorry that you feel that way."

- "Why are you so upset? It is no big deal!"

- "I need time to be alone to think."

- "I do not know how I feel; I am just not feeling the chemistry between us."

- "You are overreacting!"

- Give the attached partner the silent treatment.

Doing these things will make your partner feel like you are dismissing their feelings, and it may trigger them. The following are examples of what to say or do:

- "It will be alright; we will somehow get through this."

- "Let me give you a hug; everything will be alright."

- "I am not afraid of your feelings; I want you to tell me how you feel."

- "I may not understand why you feel this way, but I do know what it feels like to be overwhelmed. What can I do to be there for you?"

- Verify that you understand what they are saying and tell them it is important to you.

- Let them cry and hold them.

- Assure them that you care about them.

- Be consistent in giving them your attention.

- Follow through with your commitments and promises.

- Encourage them to engage in techniques of self-awareness and self-reflection.

Making statements and actions like these will pave the way to move beyond the conflict and find common ground. A partner with an anxious attachment style will likely be filled with self-doubt and frequently seek reassurance. For this reason, it is important to tell them how you feel about them rather than assume they know how you feel. It can also be very helpful to tell them how much you value them and your commitment to the relationship and that you are willing to accommodate their needs.

Keep Your Word

Being distrustful of others is an essential characteristic of this attachment style. It is important to keep your promise to your partner and follow through with what you tell them. For your sake, it is also important that you form clear boundaries for yourself and that your partner knows your expectations. Having said this, it is important that you consistently enforce your boundaries and expectations. It is this kind of consistency that will create trust in your partner.

Couples Therapy

Couples therapy can be valuable for both partners. The therapist will be a moderator and support you and your partner in communicating your feelings for each other. The two of you will also learn new communication tools.

What to do if you are in an Anxious and Avoidant Relationship

As noted before, when an anxious individual enters a relationship with an avoidant partner, they will feed off each other's weaknesses. Unless both partners are willing to change, their cycle of dysfunction will continue.

To bring about change, both partners need to follow the same course of action. They need to become conscious of their needs and feelings and be willing to risk what they fear the most.

To bring about change requires that they become conscious of their coping behaviors and resist their compulsions to cling to or avoid each other. To do all of this takes a great deal of courage.

In place of their old ways of relating to each other, the couple needs to learn to acknowledge and accept the emotions that come about when they feel stressed by the relationship. Needless to say, this kind of endeavor should be done with a trained therapist as it can be a difficult journey, especially in the beginning.

When difficult emotions arise, they may trigger feelings of rage, despair, terror, shame, and emptiness. A therapist can help you navigate these emotions and keep them apart from your current circumstances as an adult whose emotional survival is no longer at risk. As the partners work through their feelings, they will become less reactive toward them and develop a more solid sense of self.

By the couple developing and understanding their attachment styles, they learn from each other and learn to embrace the parts of themselves that they had repressed. The anxious partner can learn to set limits for themselves and care for their own needs. In contrast, the avoidant partner can learn to become more adaptable, reach out to others, and empathize with others' feelings.

The anxious partner can learn to say "no," and reduce the impact of separation anxiety, while the avoidant partner can learn to express their feelings to their partner. Ultimately, each partner learns to take responsibility for themselves. They learn to listen to each other empathetically while respecting their own needs and negotiating an agreement. In other words, they learn to compromise.

If you do not have the cooperation of your partner, there are things that you can do as an individual. Start focusing on yourself by getting to know who you are. Get to know your fears and insecurities and embrace them. Instead of seeing them as flaws, learn how you can use them to your benefit. This exploration can be done through professional therapy, meditation, or journaling. In the next chapter, we will examine some studies on the anxious attachment style.

Chapter 7

Research on the Anxious Attachment Style

The following are some studies that have been conducted on the anxious attachment style. Their results can provide insight into how you can better cope with your attachment style.

Gratitude: A New Way to Deal with Anxious Attachment?

The driving force behind the anxious attachment style is the fear of abandonment. This fear leads to thoughts and behaviors that undercut the building of trust and emotional intimacy. With that in mind, German researchers may have found a valuable tool for overcoming the destructive influences of this attachment style. That tool is gratitude.

Researchers studied the results from a long-term study that tracked romantic couples yearly for a period of over seven years. The study measured the anxiety attachment among couples by asking them to rate their level of agreement with various statements, such as:

- Sometimes, I think my partner does not enjoy being with me as much as I enjoy being with them.

- I frequently think that my partner thinks less of me when I make a mistake.

  They also measured the couple's level of gratitude for each other by asking them questions like:

- How frequently does your partner recognize you for what you have done?

- How frequently does your partner express their appreciation for you?

Besides these questions, the couples were also rated on their overall satisfaction with their relationship.

The researchers set out to see if there was a change in these factors over time. What they found surprised them. Partners who measured high for the anxiety attachment style experienced a significant decline in anxiety from a year later. What led to the decline was the experience of gratitude from their partners. But that was not all. The researchers also found that the reverse was not true. Lower levels of anxiety were not a predictor of increased gratitude later on.

The studies suggest that gratitude plays a role in reducing stress within a relationship caused by an anxious attachment style. The researchers believe that partners with an anxious attachment style develop a sense of self-worth and competence when they receive appreciation and recognition from their partners.

A partner's acts of kindness can meet the needs of an anxious partner by making them feel that they are valued in the relationship. The researchers concluded that other factors may have played a role in reducing anxiety; however, these changes were not simply the result of the partners feeling more satisfied with each other. Whether relationship satisfaction increased or decreased, the receiving of their partner's gratitude created a decline in stress in the anxious partner.

This study supports one of the recommendations by experts for changing an anxious attachment style, which is to form a relationship with someone with a secure attachment style. Those with a secure attachment style have the confidence to share their feelings and express love and affection. So, if you have a partner who has an anxious attachment style, make sure to express your gratitude for them, as long as it is sincere.

The Research: It Does Not Take Much!

Studies have shown that a change in attachment style can occur through positive experiences of closeness and intimacy. One study involved 70 heterosexual couples who participated in a survey regarding their relationship. The couples were then placed into two groups. The first group engaged in activities that promoted greater intimacy and closeness.

These couples took turns answering a series of questions about themselves. The questions selected by the researchers had been proven to enhance feelings of closeness. Another activity this group got involved in was partner yoga, a form of yoga that involved holding hands or other forms of physical contact while creating poses.

The second group engaged in activities that involved answering impersonal questions and individual yoga. After completing their exercises, the participants assessed the quality of their relationships.

Those in the first group, who were identified as having an avoidant style, rated the quality of their relationship higher than they did before participating in the activities. Those who were identified as having a secure or anxious attachment style did not show any change in how they perceived their relationship. This study appears to show that activities that build intimacy may be a benefit for those with an avoidant attachment style.

What is remarkable is that there was a follow-up on the participants one month later. The increase in the satisfaction that the avoidant style participants reported was still there. The study also revealed similar results in couples engaged in spontaneous home interactions. In this study, 67 heterosexual couples in a long-term relationship were asked to keep a diary daily for three weeks. They were told to record their feelings and their partner's behavior toward them.

The study's results found that when the romantic partners of the participants behaved positively toward them, they experienced positive emotions more frequently and negative ones less frequently. They were also happier about their relationship. Positive behaviors by the romantic partners included loving behaviors and listening to the other partner.

These findings were most evident in participants with an avoidant attachment. These studies suggest that those with an avoidant attachment style are more likely to benefit from a positive relationship than the other insecure styles.

What is encouraging about these studies is that they show that a shift to a more secure attachment style can take place by taking action that involves little time or effort. Another study found that those with an avoidant attachment style could reduce the magnitude of their negative emotions by just reflecting on positive relationship memories.

For those with an anxious attachment style, forming a relationship with someone with a secure attachment style has been beneficial in developing a more secure attachment style. Also, healing oneself from codependency is important in achieving a more secure style.

Suggested areas to work on for those with an anxious attachment style include:

- Overcoming feelings of shame and improving your self-esteem. Doing these things will keep you from personalizing others' actions of behaviors.

- Learning to become assertive.

- Learning to identify and honor the emotions you experience. Also, learn to express your emotional needs assertively.

- Develop the courage to risk being authentic and direct with your partner instead of playing games or manipulating them.

- Learning to accept others and yourself instead of focusing on the flaws.

- Learning what your triggers are and how to manage them.

- Learn to self-soothe. There are many resources on how to nurture yourself.

- Learn how to compromise and deal with conflict in a way that offers a win-win solution.

Those with an anxious attachment style should become more responsible for themselves. It is recommended that they engage in self-care and learn to nurture themselves. Also important is that they learn to take things slow when dating.

Those who are avoidant would do well to become more attentive to their partner's needs. It would be valuable for them to reveal their vulnerability, acknowledge their need for love, learn to receive, and set their boundaries verbally. Working on these things will cultivate a more secure and interdependent relationship.

It is important to point out that creating change for both insecure attachment styles means facing the fear of becoming dependent on someone. This is especially true after ending a codependent relationship. However, such fears normally come from being in a codependent relationship where neither partner has a secure attachment. A healthy dependency leads to greater interdependence by entering a secure relationship.

The fear of becoming dependent on another person can also arise when seeking therapy. In this case, it is the fear of becoming dependent on the therapist. If you experience this, you would be wise to address this fear with your therapist, as this would be a teaching moment to learn how to manage your fear.

Addressing the fear of dependency with a therapist offers the opportunity to develop the skills needed to handle such situations if they arise in the future with a partner. It is here that the paradox lies. Rather than becoming more dependent, quality therapy can help the individual develop a more secure attachment style, leading to greater autonomy. The greater our own autonomy, the more we will be able of becoming emotionally intimate with others.

Can You Change Your Attachment Style?

Can you change your attachment style? The answer to that question appears to be "no" and "yes." The literature agrees that we cannot change from one style to another; however, we can alter our attachment style to become more or less secure.

The following are three scenarios that illustrate how a life situation can change one's attachment style:

Scenario 1:

A child grows up in a loving and supportive home and develops a secure attachment style. Having a secure attachment style, he learns to trust others and is comfortable with emotional intimacy.

When he gets older, he starts to date. Unfortunately, he experiences a series of disappointing and unhealthy relationships. His partners have insecure attachment styles. They cheat on him, lie to him, or monitor his communications on his social media accounts and cell phone.

Repeated relationships of this kind destroy his confidence, resulting in him adopting a more insecure attachment style. He moves toward the avoidant end of the attachment style spectrum.

Scenario 2:

A woman has an anxious attachment style and is in a relationship where she always feels like she is on shaky ground. She forever fears that her partner will leave or that he is cheating on her. The relationship eventually breaks up. Tired of living this way, she gets therapy and works on herself.

Her efforts pay off, and she meets someone new. Her relationship with her new partner is more characteristic of a secure attachment style. She rarely experiences feelings of anxiety or jealousy. When she does, she knows how to deal with it healthily.

Scenario 3:

A man has an anxious attachment style. Because of this, his relationships are characterized by the constant need for validation from his partners. He decides to go to therapy and spends a lot of time working on himself. Later, he enters a new relationship. He eventually realizes his partner has an insecure attachment style. Instead of reverting to his anxious attachment style, he interacts with his partner more securely.

Research also shows that attachments may change over time as we get older. It is theorized that as we age, we tend to have a lower tolerance for relationships that do not meet our needs, as we have less time. Conversely, major life events can cause a secure attachment style to change to an insecure style. Examples of such events include divorce, loss of a child, and major accidents.

Image of Self and Others

Psychologists have developed a hypothetical model that demonstrates how our attachment style relates to our self-image and the image that we have of others. Those with a secure attachment style have a positive self-image and tend to view others positively.

Those with an anxious attachment style generally have a negative self-image but have a positive perception of others. This causes them to engage in needy behaviors. Individuals with an avoidant attachment style have a positive image of themselves but hold a negative one of others. This is demonstrated by an arrogant attitude and fear of commitment.

Researchers believe that these models can be helpful to those with an insecure attachment to navigate toward a more secure attachment style. The following are examples:

> Those with an anxious attachment style can work on themselves by building a more positive image and creating healthy boundaries for themselves.

> For those who are dating, discover what you are passionate about, or look toward what you are good at. Make these things your focus instead of dating. By making these adjustments, you will develop greater awareness of the self-image of those you date. You will be better equipped to find people to date who are healthier for you.

> Research shows that those with an anxious attachment style are more likely to make empowering changes when they surround themselves with healthy relationships that provide a positive emotional experience. This is particularly true when the relationship is a significant one, such as a spouse. Such relationship changes can reshape the anxious type's view of

the world, reduce their anxiety, and model what a secure attachment style looks like.

The next chapter contains guided meditations and affirmations to assist you in reaching a more secure attachment style.

CHAPTER 8

Guided Meditations and Affirmations

Going from an anxious attachment style to one that is more secure entails creating a new mindset where you have more empowering beliefs about yourself and others. Meditation is a powerful tool for reprogramming your mind to achieve such a mindset.

About Meditation

The purpose of meditation is to redirect your attention from the outer world and toward the inner world. Your experience of the world around you is a projection of how you experience your inner one. By changing your inner experience, you will experience a change in how you perceive yourself and others.

In its purest form, meditation involves going within and silently observing one's mental activity, including thoughts, perceptions, and sensations. Through this silent observation, one develops greater discernment about the nature of one's mental activity and sense of self.

When meditating, one learns how to navigate thoughts and emotions without getting caught up in them. Doing this is liberating as we no longer give our unquestioned allegiance to what our minds tell us.

There are some key points to keep in mind when learning how to meditate:

1. Maintain an attitude of total acceptance and non-judgment for everything you experience.

2. Do not try to control, change, or resist anything you experience.

3. Allow all that you experience the complete freedom to express itself.

4. When meditating, you may experience thoughts such as:

   a. My thoughts keep coming; they are not slowing down.

   b. This is too difficult.

   c. This is boring.

   d. I have more important things to do.

   e. This is not working.

   f. Am I doing this right?

Ignore these thoughts and continue to focus on meditation.

What is Guided Meditation?

Guided meditation is a meditation that follows guidance or a script. Unlike regular meditation, guided meditation guides you to a specific outcome. In other words, guided meditation is like meditation with guardrails to keep you going in a specific direction. In the case of this book, that direction leads toward developing a more secure attachment style!

Requirements: To listen to the guided meditation and receive the full benefits, you will need to download the audio version of this book on Audible. You may alternatively record the script with your own voice on your phone by reciting the words in a calming tone and following the pauses.

Guided Meditation: Before Getting Started

Guided meditation leads you on a journey within. Think of any guidance you receive as a sign on the road. The sign is not the destination; it only serves as a pointer of which direction to go. Far more important than any guidance is what you experience. What you experience while practicing is ultimately what's most important.

You may ask yourself, "But what am I supposed to be experiencing?" The answer to this question is simple. Whatever you are experiencing at any given moment is what you are supposed to be experiencing. This statement is illuminated by the following guidelines for learning to meditate:

- Have unconditional acceptance of anything that you experience. This means that you do not try to change, modify, or resist anything that appears in your awareness. Accept all thoughts, perceptions, and sensations that you experience. Yes, even if your thoughts are racing, let them be. Do not try to control them.

- Do not have any expectations about what you should be or should not be experiencing. Fully accept both yourself and what you are experiencing.

People have trouble meditating mainly because they lack acceptance of what is happening and attempt to control their minds. Instead, be like a birdwatcher observing a rare bird. For the birdwatcher, just observing the bird is a privilege.

A good bird watcher does not intrude on the bird being observed. The birdwatcher allows the bird to behave freely on its own accord. As one who is learning to meditate, you are the bird watcher. What you are experiencing is the bird. You will now start with the first guided meditation, which addresses the body's sensations.

Mindfulness of the Sensations of the Body

Our bodies experience innumerable sensations. Because we are so distracted in our daily lives, we are often unaware of them. Those of us with an anxious attachment style are often unaware of our bodily sensations until we are triggered by something. When this happens, we often get caught up in the unpleasant sensations, which leads us to lose ourselves in our emotions. This mindfulness exercise will help you develop greater awareness of the sensations of your body.

1. Lie down on the floor or on a mat (Using your bed for this exercise is discouraged as you may fall asleep.) **Pause 5 seconds**

2. Place your attention on the movement of your breath as you inhale and exhale.

Pause 3 seconds

3. As you follow your breath, become aware of the sensations of your body. Do you detect a tingling in your feet or hands? Do you sense pressure or stiffness in your back, shoulders, or neck?

4. Allow yourself to experience every sensation that you are aware of. Do not try to change them, ignore them, or judge them as being good or bad. Simply allow yourself to experience them.

Pause 3 seconds

5. Notice that the sensations you feel are not stable as they constantly change in their degree of intensity. In contrast, some sensations may seem to appear, disappear, and then reappear.

Pause 3 seconds

6. Allow yourself to experience any given sensation for as long as you desire. When you are ready, just move on to another sensation. Be sure to continue breathing as you perform this exercise.

Pause 10 seconds

7. Continue to practice this exercise as long as you wish.

By practicing this meditation, you will develop greater awareness of your body's sensations. By becoming more aware of your sensations, you avoid getting caught up in them as you will not be caught off guard.

Guided Meditation for Relaxing

Just as it is important to be aware of the sensations of your body, it is also important to know how to enter a relaxed state. Knowing how to enter a relaxed state can lower your anxiety level.

1. Take a deep breath and slowly let it out.

    Pause 3 seconds

2. Take another deep breath and slowly let it out.

    Pause 3 seconds

3. Now take a third deep breath. Hold it. Now exhale slowly.

    Pause 3 seconds

4. Now breathe normally.

    Pause 3 seconds

5. Imagine that you are on a cruise liner. You are on vacation, which is long overdue. You have worked hard for so long; now it is your time to escape.

    Pause 5 seconds

6. You are standing at the ship's bow, which is out at sea. All you can see is the vastness of the ocean and the open horizon beyond it.

    Pause 5 seconds

7. In your mind, see the endless waves that approach you and hear the gentle hum of the ship's engine.

    Pause 3 seconds

8. Sea birds hover above you, and you see an occasional dolphin leap above the waves.

9. The sights and sounds are making you feel more and more relaxed.

10. The gentle ocean breeze and salt spray leave you feeling refreshed and revived.

Pause 3 seconds

11. Take a deep breath and slowly let it out.

Pause 3 seconds

12. Now breathe normally.

Pause 3 seconds

13. Your ship is approaching its destination, an island that few know about.

14. You can see the island in the distance. The captain has informed you that this island will be your "escape from everything" and that you can spend a full day there.

15. What do you say to yourself, knowing that you are leaving the rest of the world behind you?

Pause 3 seconds

16. Take a deep breath and slowly let it out.

Pause 3 seconds

17. Now breathe normally.

Pause 3 seconds

18. Your ship is now anchored less than a mile away from the island. It is the closest that it can get because of the reefs. You board a skiff, and it takes you to the island.

19. When the skiff reaches the island, you disembark. You find yourself on a pristine and secluded beach.

20. Walking along the shore, you realize you are the only one there. There is no one around to distract you from the natural beauty surrounding you.

Pause 3 seconds

21. Feel your toes sink into the soft white sand and the sensations of the surf against your skin.

Pause 3 seconds

22. You keep on walking until you find the perfect spot to lay down your towel and do some sunbathing.

Pause 3 seconds

23. Feel the weight of your outstretched body settle on the softness of your towel and the sand.

Pause 3 seconds

24. Closing your eyes, you hear the soothing sound of the surf as it rushes up the shoreline and the occasional squawking of a seabird.

25. You feel yourself becoming more and more relaxed with the sound

of each wave that reaches the shore.

Pause 3 seconds

26. Take a deep breath and slowly let it out.

Pause 3 seconds

27. Now breathe normally.

Pause 3 seconds

28. In your mind, hear the sound of a wave. As you do so, feel your body becoming more relaxed.

Pause 3 seconds

29. Another wave arrives. Feel the stress leave your body as your thoughts evaporate under the sun.

Pause 3 seconds

30. Another wave approaches and feel yourself going deeper and deeper into relaxation.

Pause 3 seconds

31. Notice that your breathing is becoming deeper and fuller.

Pause 3 seconds

32. Feeling fully relaxed, you get up from your towel and walk toward the shore.

33. You wade into the surf and feel the warm turquoise waters against

your skin.

34. While bathing in the tropical waters, you look around.

35. In your mind, see the lush green jungles further up the beach.

36. See the endless blue horizon as you look out toward the sea.

37. Notice how free your body feels as the warm, clear waters support you.

Pause 3 seconds

38. Now, take a deep breath and slowly let it out.

Pause 3 seconds

39. Take another deep breath and slowly let it out.

Pause 3 seconds

40. How does it feel to be in a deeply relaxed state?

Pause 3 seconds

41. What do you notice when you are feeling relaxed?

42. Do you feel a certain sensation in your body?

43. How does that sensation feel?

Pause 3 seconds

44. What do you say to yourself when you are feeling very relaxed? Perhaps you do not tell yourself anything, which is very good!

Pause 3 seconds

45. Now take a third deep breath. Hold it. Now exhale slowly.

Pause 3 seconds

46. Now breathe normally.

Pause 3 seconds

47. Though you may imagine that you are on a tropical island, the relaxation you experienced was created by you.

48. Know that you can relax by focusing on anything that you find peaceful.

To be good at anything in life takes practice. Getting what you want out of this meditation is no different. The more you practice this meditation, the greater the results that you experience. For this reason, it is recommended that you meditate daily.

Guided Meditation for Managing Your Emotions

It was previously explained that nothing in our experience has inherent meaning. Instead, it is we who give meaning to our experience. Emotions have a powerful effect on our lives. However, this is made possible only because we grant emotions their power. Because we are the creator of meaning in our lives, we can control the meaning we give to our experiences. The following technique can be used to manage how you feel about a situation.

Guided Meditation for Gaining Control of Negative Emotions

Emotions are a natural aspect of who we are as human beings. Emotions are forms of energy that we have come to categorize as being positive or negative. Unfortunately, many of us focus on our negative emotions. Focusing on our negative emotions can lead to both mental and physical problems. In this meditation, you will be guided to understand better emotions and how to become less reactive to them.

1. Get in a comfortable position and close your eyes.

   Pause 3 seconds

2. Now, take a deep breath and hold it.

   Pause 3 seconds

3. Slowly let it out.

   Pause 3 seconds

4. Breathe normally, and relax.

   Pause 5 seconds

5. Take another deep breath. Hold it.

   Pause 5 seconds

6. Slowly let it out.

   Pause 3 seconds

7. Breathe normally, and relax.

Pause 3 seconds

8. Take another deep breath. Hold it.

Pause 5 seconds

9. Slowly let it out.

Pause 3 seconds

10. Breathe normally, and relax.

Pause 3 seconds

11. Place your attention on your breath. Make your breath the focus of your attention. Feel the sensations you experience as your breath travels in and out of your body.

Pause 5 seconds

12. Before starting this meditation, you will be guided into deeper levels of relaxation. You will hear a countdown from 10 to 1.

13. As you hear the numbers, notice and focus on the rising and falling of your abdomen as you breathe.

Pause 3 seconds

14. 10

Brief pause

15. 9

Brief pause

16. 8

Brief pause

17. 7

Brief pause

18. 6

Brief pause

19. 5

Brief pause

20. 4

Brief pause

21. 3

Brief pause

22. 2

Brief pause

23. 1

Pause 3 seconds

24. Feel yourself becoming very relaxed

Pause 3 seconds

25. Put your attention on your breath as it travels through your body.

Pause 3 seconds

26. Focus on the sensations that you experience as you breathe in and out.

Pause 3 seconds

27. Feel the weight of your body as you go deeper and deeper into relaxation.

Pause 3 seconds

28. As you relax, you will experience thoughts, emotions, and perceptions

Pause 3 seconds

29. These are natural phenomena that are part of your existence.

Pause 3 seconds

30. You are about to explore the nature of emotions. Any realizations that you make regarding your emotions can be applied to your thoughts and perceptions.

Pause 3 seconds

31. Notice what you are feeling right now.

32. If you are unable to identify the emotion, that is okay. Developing a deeper understanding of emotions does not require you to have the correct term for them.

33. Just ask yourself what the emotion feels like. Does it feel negative, neutral, or positive?

Pause 3 seconds

34. Treat the emotion you are experiencing as though it was a rare bird, and you are the bird watcher.

Pause 3 seconds

35. The bird watcher does not intrude upon the bird or alter its behavior.

Pause 3 seconds

36. Similarly, do not try to change, control, or resist any emotion you experience.

Pause 3 seconds

37. To observe an emotion is to be aware of its existence.

Pause 3 seconds

38. You are about to be asked a series of questions about what you are experiencing.

39. When answering these questions, do not resort to logic or your imagination. Instead, go by your direct experience.

Pause 3 seconds

40. What can you observe about the emotion that you are experiencing?

41. Does it have a color?

Pause 3 seconds

42. Does it have a size?

Pause 3 seconds

43. Does it have a shape?

Pause 3 seconds

44. Where is it located?

Pause 3 seconds

45. Is the emotion you are experiencing confined to a specific space, or is it without boundaries?

Pause 3 seconds

46. Is the emotion you are experiencing fixed and permanent, or is it continuously changing in its level of intensity?

Pause 3 seconds

47. As you observe the emotion, is it causing any problems for you?

Pause 3 seconds

48. Take another deep breath. Hold it.

Pause 5 seconds

49. Slowly let it out.

Pause 3 seconds

50. Breathe normally, and relax.

Pause 3 seconds

51. Now think of a time in the past when you experienced this emotion.

Pause 5 seconds

52. Recall the situation as vividly as you can.

Pause 5 seconds

53. Can you determine what triggered its appearance?

Pause 3 seconds

54. How did experiencing this emotion then differ from what you are experiencing now?

Pause 3 seconds

55. If you feel less impacted than you did in the past, it is because you are aware of the emotion without engaging with it.

Pause 3 seconds

56. You got curious about it rather than getting caught up on it.

Pause 3 seconds

57. Now say to yourself, "My emotions have no power over me unless I allow them to." When you say it, say it with meaning. Do it now.

Pause 3 seconds

58. Now say again, "My emotions have no power over me unless I allow them to." When you say it, say it with conviction. Do it now.

Pause 3 seconds

59. Emotions possess no power of their own. You give emotions their power by getting caught up in them.

Pause 3 seconds

60. Accept whatever emotion enters your awareness.

Pause 3 seconds

61. Observe them with curiosity without losing yourself in them.

Pause 3 seconds

62. You will now hear a count from 1 to 5.

63. With each count, you will become more awake.

1... Feel yourself beginning to awake.

2... Experience your mind becoming more active.

3...Feel your body becoming more energized.

4... Move your hands, feet, and neck.

5... Open your eyes and feel refreshed.

Pause 3 seconds

64. Take as long as you want to savor your experience before getting up.

Emotions are a natural aspect of who we are. Further, there are no good or bad emotions. It is we who give meaning to emotions. Learn to accept all of your emotions as you would accept a guest. When you accept your so-called negative emotions, they will lose their power over you. Practice this meditation daily until you can do this.

Guided Meditation for Transforming your Emotions

In this meditation, you will transform a negative emotion into a positive or neutral one. This meditation will require that you stay present while experiencing negative emotions.

1. Sit down in a comfortable position and close your eyes.

2. Follow your breath during inhalation and exhalation. Focus on your breath; feel it as it courses through your body.

3. Now think about a situation that concerns you. As you think of this situation, observe the emotions and sensations that arise from within you.

4. Now ask yourself, "What does this situation mean to me?" As you respond to this question, pay attention to the feelings that you are experiencing.

5. Now ask yourself, "What I am experiencing, what does it feel like?" For example, you may be experiencing tension. Using this example, the next question you would ask yourself would be, "What does tension feel like?" Continuing with the example, I

would say that tension feels constricted and heavy.

6. Notice that the question was not what you think about tension; do not involve your thoughts in this process. Ask yourself, "What does it FEEL like?" Get in touch with what your experience FEELS like. Also, do not doubt yourself; go with the first answer that comes to you. Do not worry about your words; focus on identifying the feeling. Make sure that you continue to breathe as you experience the feeling. Allow yourself to dive into it.

7. Whatever your response was to the last question, ask yourself, "What does that feel like?" Going back to the previous example, if tension feels like my body is constricted and heavy, the next question I would ask myself is, "What does be constricted and heavy feel like?" Continuing with my example, I would say, "Being constricted and heavy feels like I am being crushed by a boulder." Whatever answer you receive, get in touch with its feeling. Making sure that you continue to breathe as you experience the feeling.

8. Whatever your response was to the last question, ask yourself, "What does that feel like?" If my response were that being constricted and heavy feels like I am being crushed by a boulder, I would then ask myself, "What does be crushed by a boulder feel like?"

9. The format for this exercise is to repeatedly ask yourself, "What does it feel like?" After asking the question, dive into the feeling and fully experience it. As always, continue to breathe.

10. When you continuously ask these questions and allow yourself to experience the feelings fully, the feeling will transform on its own.

11. You will know when you reach the end when the previously unpleasant feeling is now pleasant or neutral.

12. You can also use this same meditation on positive emotions, in which case, the positive feeling of the emotion will expand.

13. Repeat this exercise until you can successfully transform a negative emotion. Just for clarification, emotions are not positive or negative; they feel negative or positive by the meaning we give them. This is why this meditation works; you are giving your emotions attention without imposing judgment on them.

The last exercise was intended to transform negative emotions. In the next exercise, you will learn how to harness positive emotions. This exercise can be used to experience any positive emotion that you desire. In explaining this exercise, the emotion of happiness is used.

1. Get in a comfortable position and relax.

2. Close your eyes, take a deep breath, and then let it out slowly.

3. Now think of a time when you were the happiest.

4. Now go back to that memory when you were the happiest.

5. Where were you at that time?

6. Make your memory as clear and detailed as possible as you think of that place.

7. As you think about that time, notice how you feel.

8. Focus on the feeling and try to intensify it. When you reach peak intensity, say to yourself your favorite color or number.

9. Now go back to that memory again. What were you doing at that time that made you happy?

10. Make your memory as clear and detailed as possible as you reflect on what you were doing.

11. As you think about what you were doing, notice how you feel.

12. Focus on the feeling and try to intensify it. When you reach peak intensity, say to yourself your favorite color or number.

13. Now go back to that memory again. Who was around you when you did that thing that made you happy?

14. Make your memory as clear and detailed as possible as you think back to who was around you.

15. As you think about that time, notice how you feel.

16. Focus on the feeling and try to intensify it. When you reach peak intensity, say to yourself your favorite color or number.

17. Now go back to that memory again. When you were doing that thing that made you happy, what did you see?

18. Make your memory as clear and detailed as possible as you think back to what you saw.

19. As you think about that time, notice how you feel.

20. Focus on the feeling and try to intensify it. When you reach peak intensity, say to yourself your favorite color or number.

21. Now go back to that memory again. What did you hear when you were doing that thing that made you happy?

22. Make your memory as clear and detailed as possible as you think back to what you heard.

23. As you think about that time, notice how you feel.

24. Focus on the feeling and try to intensify it. When you reach peak intensity, say to yourself your favorite color or number.

25. Now go back to that memory again. Did you taste or smell something when you were doing something that made you happy?

26. If so, make your memory as clear and detailed as possible as you reflect on what you smelled or tasted.

27. As you think about that time, notice how you feel.

28. Focus on the feeling and try to intensify it. When you reach peak intensity, say to yourself your favorite color or number.

29. Now open your eyes. Say to yourself your favorite color or number. Do you feel a change in how you feel? Keep practicing this exercise until saying your favorite color or number brings about your desired emotion.

Practice these last two meditations until you experience their transformative powers. Keep practicing; it will be worth it! You will harness the emotions you desire and reduce the potency of those emotions you do not want to experience.

Guided Visualization

An insecure attachment style is like a bad habit when it no longer serves us. One way to change your habits is to go straight to the subconscious level through visualization. When first learning how to tie your shoes or drive a car, odds are that you were not very good at it. Learning to do these things took a lot of concentration and practice. The more you practiced doing these things, the more effective you became. There came a point when you did not even have to think about how to do these things because they were ingrained in your subconscious.

When changing a habit, you need to replace it with a new one and practice it over and over. However, rehearsing the new behavior does not have to occur exclusively in the real world. You can also rehearse the new behaviors in your mind. By visualizing in your mind the new behaviors that you want to adopt, you can speed up the time that it takes for them to become part of your life.

Visualizing is simple if you keep this in mind: everyone visualizes differently. While some people see vivid images, others see murky ones. Both of these are fine. When visualizing, trust whatever it is that you are experiencing.

1. Think of a minor change that you would like to make. You want to start small. Using visualization, you can deal with the bigger changes when you become more experienced.

2. When you have identified the change that you wish to make, get into a relaxed state. You can focus on your breath, or meditate.

3. When you are relaxed, visualize yourself in a situation where you want to change your behavior. For example, if you want to be

more assertive, visualize yourself in a situation where you want to express how you feel. Make your visualizations as detailed as you can.

4. Imagine yourself being how you want to be. If you want to be more assertive, see yourself becoming more assertive.

5. As you visualize yourself being how you want to be, incorporate your five senses. When you are being assertive, what do you see? What do you feel when you are being this new you? Do you hear anything? Do you sound differently when you speak? Do you smell or taste anything?

Practice visualization twice a day for a few minutes. Also, bolster your visualization practice with real world practice. You can do that by committing to a plan. For example, you will practice being assertive anytime you feel a need to express yourself.

Guided Meditations for Relationships

Healthy relationships begin with partners that are emotionally aware of themselves. They also seek to be emotionally supportive of their partners. The following guided meditations address these points.

Guided Meditation for Healing Your Relationships with Others

No relationship is free from upsets or disagreements. When this happens, it is easy for our emotions to take charge and make things worse. The following meditation provides a way to begin to heal relationship wounds.

1. Sit down in a comfortable position and close your eyes.

Pause 3 seconds

2. Now breathe deeply, hold your breath briefly, then exhale.

Pause 3 seconds

3. Feel the relaxation in your body.

Pause 3 seconds

4. Feel yourself becoming more and more relaxed.

Pause 3 seconds

5. Follow your breath during inhalation and exhalation. Place your attention on your breath. Feel it as it courses through your body.

Pause 3 seconds

6. You are about to be asked to recall a memory. Know that you are safe and protected. When you recall the memory, imagine that it is a movie and that you are watching it from the audience.

Pause 3 seconds

7. I want you to think of someone you believe treated you unfairly or unjustly. It can be recent or from the past. When you have this person in mind, I want you to relive the specific situation where this person mistreated you.

Pause 3 seconds

8. Where did the situation take place?

Pause 5 seconds

9. What were the surroundings like? What did you see?

Pause 5 seconds

10. Where was this person when the situation happened?

Pause 5 seconds

11. What were they doing at the time?

Pause 5 seconds

12. See it in your mind; visualize it in as much detail as possible.

Pause 10 seconds

13. Where were you at the time?

Pause 3 seconds

14. What were you doing when the situation happened?

Pause 3 seconds

15. What did they say or do to you that caused you to be angry or hurt?

Pause 3 seconds

16. How did you feel when it happened?

Pause 3 seconds

17. What did you tell yourself?

Pause 3 seconds

18. Now breathe deeply, hold your breath briefly, then exhale.

Pause 3 seconds

19. Feel the relaxation in your body.

Pause 3 seconds

20. Feel yourself becoming more and more relaxed.

Pause 3 seconds

21. Follow your breath during inhalation and exhalation. Place your attention on your breath. Feel it as it courses through your body.

Pause 3 seconds

22. Feel yourself getting more and more relaxed.

Pause 3 seconds

23. I want you to replay the situation in your mind a second time. This time I want you to observe this person without judgment. Observe the situation objectively.

Pause 3 seconds

24. Where did the situation take place?

Pause 5 seconds

25. What were the surroundings like? What did you see?

Pause 5 seconds

26. Where was this person when the situation happened?

Pause 5 seconds

27. What were they doing at the time?

Pause 5 seconds

28. See it in your mind; visualize it in as much detail as possible.

Pause 10 seconds

29. Where were you at the time? What were you doing when the situation happened?

Pause 3 seconds

30. What did they say or do to you that caused you to be angry or hurt?

Pause 3 seconds

31. Now ask yourself: "Am I 100% positive that this person intended to hurt me?"

Pause 5 seconds

32. Also, ask yourself: "Is there any chance I misinterpreted the situation?"

Pause 3 seconds

33. Ask yourself: "Is it possible that I am projecting my thoughts and emotions on this person?"

Pause 5 seconds

34. Now ask yourself this question: "This thing that I am accusing this person of, is it possible that I am doing the same thing to myself by holding on to these emotions?

Pause 5 seconds

35. If this is true for you, ask yourself, "How can I be more loving toward myself?"

Pause 5 seconds

36. Now breathe deeply, hold your breath briefly, then exhale.

Pause 3 seconds

37. Feel the relaxation in your body.

Pause 3 seconds

38. Feel yourself becoming more and more relaxed.

Pause 3 seconds

39. Follow your breath during inhalation and exhalation. Place your attention on your breath.

Pause 3 seconds

40. We can only behave at the level of awareness that we are at. If we were at higher levels of awareness, we would make different choices. Now say to yourself: "I am healing my relationships through compassion for myself and others." When you say it, say it with

meaning. Say it now.

Pause 5 seconds

41. Say it again, with even more conviction: "I am healing my relationships through compassion for myself and others." Experience what you feel when you say this. Say it now.

Pause 5 seconds

42. One last time, say it with the meaning: "I am healing my relationships through compassion for myself and others." Experience what you feel when you say this. Say it now.

Pause 5 seconds

43. Now breathe deeply, hold your breath briefly, then exhale.

Pause 3 seconds

44. Feel the relaxation in your body.

Pause 3 seconds

45. Feel yourself becoming more and more relaxed.

Pause 3 seconds

46. We attract into our lives that which matches our intentions. However, our intentions need to be pure and based on the desire that everyone involved benefits.

Pause 3 seconds

47. The statement "I am healing my relationships through compassion

for myself and others" is an intention. Our intentions can manifest into reality when we release our intention while experiencing a quiet mind.

Pause 2 seconds

48. Now breathe normally. As you breathe, place your attention on your breath. Notice the sensations you experience as your breath travels into and out of your body.

Pause 3 seconds

49. Feel yourself becoming more and more relaxed. Enjoy the feeling.

Pause 2 seconds

50. Continue to follow your breath as it enters and leaves your body.

Pause 2 seconds

51. Feel yourself becoming more and more relaxed.

Pause 2 seconds

52. Accept everything that enters your awareness without any judgment.

Pause 2 seconds

53. Become more and more relaxed.

Pause 2 seconds

54. Feel yourself going deeper and deeper within. Allow yourself to surrender to everything that you experience.

Pause 5 seconds

55. Continue to breathe and remain aware of the flow of your breath.

Pause 2 seconds

56. Now make the intention: "I am healing my relationships through compassion for myself and others." Do not hold on to this intention. As soon as you are aware of it, let it go. Release your intention to the universe.

Pause 2 seconds

57. By letting go, you allow the universe to organize the situations and events that will support you in making your intention a reality.

Pause 5 seconds

58. I will guide you in coming out of your meditative state. When you awake, know that you will be guided by life toward achieving your intention each day. Treat each experience as a teacher who is there to point the way.

   I will now count to five. With each count, you will come closer to exiting your meditative state:

   1. Feel yourself beginning to awake.

   2. Experience your mind becoming more active.

   3. Feel your body becoming more energized.

   4. Move your hands, feet, and neck.

5. Open your eyes and feel refreshed.

6. This is the end of this exercise.

Guided Meditation for Relationship Success

1. Sit down in a comfortable position and close your eyes.

Pause 3 seconds

2. Now breathe deeply, hold your breath briefly, then exhale.

Pause 3 seconds

3. Feel the relaxation in your body.

Pause 3 seconds

4. Feel yourself becoming more and more relaxed.

Pause 3 seconds

5. Follow your breath during inhalation and exhalation. Place your attention on your breath. Feel it as it courses through your body.

Pause 3 seconds.

6. I want you to visualize the person that you want a relationship with. In your mind, see their face and hear their voice.

Pause 5 seconds.

7. As you think about this person, notice any feelings that may appear.

Pause 5 seconds.

8. Now imagine yourself talking to this person. See yourself being confident and relaxed as you talk to them.

Pause 3 seconds.

9. See yourself and this person enjoying each other's company. Also, see yourself not having any expectations as you converse with them. Just enjoy the moment.

Pause 3 seconds.

10. Now imagine that you and this person are on a date. You are dining in a restaurant and have your private booth. You have an enjoyable conversation. As you get to know this person, what are some of their needs? What are they looking for?

Pause 5 seconds.

11. What can they offer you? What needs of yours can they meet?

Pause 5 seconds

12. Now ask yourself what you can offer this person. What can you give to them?

Pause 5 seconds

13. Now breathe deeply, hold your breath briefly, then exhale.

Pause 3 seconds

14. Feel the relaxation in your body.

Pause 3 seconds

15. The exchange that you just experienced occurred in your mind. Though this is obvious, what is less evident is that everything we experience originates from the mind.

Pause 2 seconds

16. Everything we see, hear, smell, taste, and touch is an interpretation our brain makes. Our senses take in information from the environment and convert it into electrical impulses. Our brains interpret this information. When we have an experience, we experience an interpretation that we created.

Pause 2 seconds

17. Your brain cannot distinguish between an actual date or you imagining one. Everything that you experience in this meditation is a projection of your mind.

Pause 2 seconds

18. Relationship success comes from learning to accept yourself, including your perceived flaws fully.

Pause 2 seconds

19. You are perfect just the way you are. It is when we have a lack of self-acceptance that we create resistance within ourselves. It is this resistance that prevents us from experiencing relationship success.

Pause 3 seconds

20. Now breathe deeply, hold your breath briefly, then exhale.

Pause 3 seconds

21. Feel the relaxation in your body.

Pause 3 seconds

22. Feel yourself becoming more and more relaxed.

Pause 5 seconds

23. Now say to yourself: "I fully accept myself as I am."

Pause 3 seconds

24. Say it again, with even more conviction: "I fully accept myself as I am."

Pause 3 seconds

25. Experience what you feel when you say this.

Pause 5 seconds

26. One last time, say it with meaning: "I fully accept myself as I am." Experience what you feel when you say this.

Pause 3 seconds

27. Now breathe normally. As you breathe, place your attention on your breath. Notice the sensations you experience as your breath travels into and out of your body.

Pause 3 seconds

28. Feel yourself becoming more and more relaxed.

Pause 3 seconds

29. Accept everything that enters your awareness without any judgment.

Pause 2 seconds

30. Become more and more relaxed.

Pause 2 seconds

31. Feel yourself going deeper and deeper within. Allow yourself to surrender to everything that you experience.

Pause 5 seconds

32. Continue to breathe and remain aware of the flow of your breath.

Pause 2 seconds

33. Now make the intention "I fully accept myself as I am."

Pause 2 seconds

34. Do not hold on to this intention. As soon as you are aware of it, let it go. Release your intention to the universe.

Pause 2 seconds

35. By letting go, you allow the universe to organize the situations and events that will support you in making your intention a reality.

Pause 5 seconds

36. I will guide you in coming out of your meditative state. When you awake, know that you will be guided by life toward achieving your

intention each day. Treat each experience as a teacher who is there to point the way.

Pause 2 seconds

37. I will now count to five. With each count, you will come closer to exiting your meditative state:

   1... Feel yourself beginning to awake.

   2... Experience your mind becoming more active.

   3...Feel your body becoming more energized.

   4... Move your hands, feet, and neck.

   5... Open your eyes and feel refreshed.

This is the end of this exercise. In the next section, we will explore the use of affirmations.

Affirmations

As with guided meditation, affirmations can also be a useful tool for creating a more secure attachment style.

How Affirmations Work

Affirmations are empowering statements we make to ourselves with a sense of conviction. By repeating affirmations, one creates a new focal point for attention. The increased attention leads to the affirmation becoming established in one's belief system.

Each time you repeat an affirmation, you strengthen your beliefs about what is true. You are also strengthening your vision of what your life can become. The reason for this is that repeating affirmations rewires your brain.

When you first start repeating affirmations, it may seem like you are just going through the motions. You may feel that nothing much is happening, that you are just repeating words.

If this is your experience, do not be disappointed, as this is normal. Repeat your affirmations as often as you like. The more you repeat them, the more ingrained they will become in your consciousness.

It takes about a month of consistently repeating affirmations before you notice any changes. One of the changes you will notice is that the affirmation will replace your limiting beliefs. Your mind will become conditioned through empowering thoughts. If a negative thought appears, your affirmation will automatically take its place.

How to Use Affirmations

To be effective, affirmations need to be experienced emotionally. Many people make the mistake of simply repeating the affirmation to themselves, which has little power. To be effective, affirmations need to be accompanied by emotional intensity. When you repeat an affirmation to yourself, say it like you mean it!

For this reason, you must choose an affirmation that you believe in. You need to believe what you are saying. If you do not believe in the affirmation, you will just be repeating words.

When reciting affirmations, you may feel a sense of calm or relief. If that is the case, you have selected an affirmation that is right for you. The following are suggestions for using affirmations:

- Choose affirmations that resonate with you. You want to select affirmations that are meaningful to you. You also want to choose an affirmation that matches the outcome you want to achieve.

- Affirmations work better when you can hear yourself speak the words. Say your affirmation out loud while standing before a mirror. Do this for five minutes, three times a day.

- You can also write out your affirmations in your journal. Writing them out or saying them aloud is superior to just thinking about them. When writing your affirmations, focus on one affirmation at a time. As with reciting your affirmation, the more you write it out, the better.

- Visualize your affirmations as though you were experiencing them in your current reality.

When visualizing, see yourself thinking and behaving consistently with your affirmation.

The following are the affirmations.

- My life is a gift for me to discover and unwrap.

- I am loved by the universe, and all of my experiences are for my pruning.

- I proudly express my beliefs and what I stand for.

- I am strong and nurturing.

- I am proud and beautiful.

- I am not a stereotype; I am a person.

- My dignity and worth as a human being are granted by my creator.

- I deserve to be here.

- I deserve the chance to make a difference in my world.

- I deserve to take up space to create a better life for m

- I am worthy of respect.

- I am worthy of an opportunity.

- I am intelligent and wise.

- I am liberating myself from the chains of my negativity.

- I am intelligent and capable.

- I am worthy because I exist.

- I am strengthened by my love for others and myself.

- I am loved. I give love. I am in love.

- I deserve all the good things that come to me.

- I take responsibility for my health.

- I take time for self-care because I am worth it.

- I take care of myself so that I can do God's work.

- I honor myself by being true to who I am.

- I have something to give to this world.

- I have something to contribute to the making of a better world.

- I celebrate life for giving me life.

- I stand up for life, for life is sacred.

- I embrace the abundance that life has to offer.

- I am a good person, and I am worthy.

- I am a source of love, strength, and faith.

- I honor and believe in myself.

- I have something to offer the world.

- I am grateful to be born into life.

- My happiness is deserved because I exist.

- I am growing as a person

- I deserve a place at the table.

- I deserve to be part of the conversation.

- I am more than enough to be successful.

- I am good enough just being me.

- I will honor my pain.

- I affirm the need to acknowledge my pain.

- I am embracing freedom, for it is my divine right.

- I validate my feelings because they are my connection to my soul.

- I am worthy of all good things in life.

- My life matters, for it, comes from the source of life itself.

- I am worthy of respect and dignity.

- I am worthy of appreciation.

- I love myself for who I am.

- I am a light of God.

- I forgive others.

- I am worthy of success.

- I am determined to be successful.

- I am committed to achieving my dreams.

- I forgive myself.

- I am committed to my success.

- I am blessed with love.

- I am blessed with faith and hope.

- I embrace love.

- I celebrate my life and the life of others.

- I am the manifestation of love.

- I am worthy of being cherished.

- How I feel is a decision that I make.

- I forgive the past and embrace the future.

- I love me.

- I love myself.

- I cherish who I am.

- I value my health.

- I am in control of my mind.

- I love myself.

- I love the way I look.

- I take care of my health, for it is a gift from my creator.

- I am powerful.

- I love living healthfully.

- I take care of myself emotionally and physically.

- I am where I am supposed to be at this moment. It is my starting point for greatness.

- I add value to this world.

- My body is healing itself of illness.

- I am creating a legacy for my loved ones.

- I take care of myself because I am worth it.

- I love challenging myself.

- I give and embrace love.

- I am breaking through the bondage of lies that I was told.

- I am passionate about living healthfully.

- I am blessed to be alive.

- I am becoming stronger and wiser.

- I am in charge of my health.

- I am focused and disciplined.

- My love and wisdom run deep.

- I am blessed with good fortune.

- I am blessed with love.

- I am becoming healthier and stronger.

- I am the captain of my destiny.

- I respect myself, and I respect life.

- I love myself and my life.

- My life is radiant; like a precious jewel, it shines.

- I am blessed with hidden talents.

- In the art of life, I am a masterpiece.

- I have everything that I need

- I am prosperous in heart and spirit.

- I am proud of who I am.

- I have boundaries because I respect myself and others.

- I am open to life.

- What I think matters.

- What I have to say matters.

- I determine how I define myself.

- I seek help because we are all connected and support each other.

- I love myself just the way I am.

- I am grateful for all of my life's experiences.

- I believe in myself because I am an expression of my creator.

- I am valuable because I have something to give.

- I am in tune with myself.

- I practice self-care.

- I am a great person because of who I am.

- I am adventurous and fun-loving.

- I am a proud and beautiful woman.

- I love being me.

- I am worthy; I deserve all good things that come to me.

- I am loved, and I love.

- I am compassionate and caring.

- I do not have to explain or justify who I am. I am worthy of respect just the way I am.

- I choose to be happy and successful.

- I have no need to impress others or to prove myself. I am worthy of happiness for just being me.

- I accept and love myself for who I am.

- I take time for myself because I deserve it.

- I am worthy of happiness.

- Today, I will believe in myself.

- I am worthy of all my desires.

- I love my hair texture. It is beautiful. It is me.

- I set boundaries for myself out of respect for myself.

- I spend time centering myself.

- I set boundaries out of respect for myself and others.

- I am a loving and supportive friend.

- I am healthy, strong, and beautiful.

- I strive for only the best for myself and others.

- I am a loving soul, and I am loved by others.

- My strength is in my vulnerability.

- I can love others because I love myself.

- I do not have to do anything to prove my self-worth.

- I belong where ever I am.

- I always win when I am myself.

- I am loved and supported by the universe.

- My worth as a woman is beyond measure.

- My self-worth is without conditions.

- I am gentle and caring with myself throughout life's changes.

- I honor my feelings, for they are valid.

- I heal myself by allowing myself to experience all that I feel.

- My gifts and individuality speak for themselves.

- I refuse to hold on to shame, for it does not serve me.

- I come closer to healing whenever I embrace my inner child.

- I will achieve my dream life by taking full responsibility for my life.

- I honor myself by taking care of myself.

- I take care of myself because I have compassion for myself.

- I take care of myself so that I can take care of others.

- I commit myself to self-care because I deserve it.

- I take play seriously because it is restorative to my life.

- I use my body in ways that bring me joy.

- I prioritize rest, for it is what keeps me going.

- By being intentional, I exert less energy but accomplish more.

- I turn my attention to my breath when life gets too busy.

- My having fun is as important as my work.

- I do not have to know other people's business to remain informed.

- I give my peace of mind the highest priority.

- My greatest treasures are peace, stillness, and simplicity.

- My inner calm repels chaos.

- I care for myself so that I can care for others.

- I am beautiful and worthy of happiness.

- I am beautiful in my own right, as are others.

- I am worthy because my life has dignity.

- Each day, I give to myself and my business.

- I deserve to take care of myself because I work hard.

- I embrace my flaws as areas of opportunity for growth.

- I honor my hopes and dreams.

- I have the right to say "no."

- I allow myself to say "no," without guilt.

- I take my time to do things correctly instead of taking shortcuts.

- I am grateful for the mind and body that I was given.

- I do not give up on myself.

- I speak my truth and uphold my dignity.

- I stand tall and take pride in myself for being who I am.

- I am learning to forgive myself and others.

- I am a human being, and I demand that I be treated as such.

- My value as a person is self-evident and immeasurable.

- I do not allow others or society to define my self-worth. My self-worth is unlimited.

- My opinion matters, and I have self-worth.

- I am worthy of respect and of giving respect.

- I deserve abundance in my life.

- I believe in myself and do not give in to the opinions of others.

- I am nurtured by the love that I have for others and myself.

- My life is rich because I deserve it.

- I take care of myself. It is my responsibility to myself and my loved ones.

- I treat self-care as being as important as caring for others.

- My body is God's temple. Self-care is my expression of appreciation.

- I learn to appreciate myself more and more with each day.

- It is in my acknowledging my pain that I begin the process of my healing

- My life and freedom are the same, and they are my divine right.

- I love and embrace myself just as I am.

- I love myself just as I am.

- I let go of guilt and embrace forgiveness for myself and others.

- Forgiveness is the healing water that washes away the residue of my guilt.

- I free myself from the shackles of guilt and shame and rise on the wings of forgiveness.

- When I embrace love, I embrace myself.

- I am the manifestation of the love that created me.

- I love myself for being me.

- I have love and compassion for myself.

- My uniqueness is the spice of my humanity.

- I care for my health because I deserve a happy life.

- I love myself unconditionally.

- I engage in self-care so that I can offer more of myself.

- I am loved because I give love.

- I am living a healthy lifestyle and feeling better about myself.

- I practice self-care because I am worth it.

- My self-worth is without limits.

- I take pride in myself.

- I celebrate my life.

- I make my health and well-being a priority.

- Being focused and disciplined is my expression of self-love.

- When I am self-disciplined, I am demonstrating self-love.

- I treat my physical well-being as a priority.

- I set boundaries out of love for myself and my respect for others.

- I, and I alone, determine how I want to be and live.

- I reach out for help when needed, for we are here to support each other.

- I love the person that I am.

- I take care of myself without guilt.

- I am a great person for being honest with whom I am.

- I love the way that I am.

- I love being who I am.

- I am worthy of all blessings that have entered my life.

- I am loved, and I love.

- I am engaged in self-care to offer value to others and myself.

- I am proud, and I do not have to justify myself for being me.

- I exhibit grace and dignity.

- I am radiant and living.

- I am happy and successful, just as I am.

- I honor my past.

- My existence matters.

- I feel no pressure to be anyone other than me.

- I embrace myself for being the person I am.

- I take care of myself because I am worth it.

- My life matters.

- I deserve happiness.

- My worthiness is beyond what I even can imagine.

- My personal happiness is more important than the expectations of others.

- My happiness is as important as anyone else's.

- How I feel matters.

- I adore how I look.

- My dreams are being realized.

- I celebrate my small victories.

- I have faith in the person who I am.

- I am deserving of all that I have received.

- I conduct myself to a higher standard.

- I am compassionate and understanding with myself.

- My body is a beautiful work of creation.

- I establish boundaries for myself as part of self-love.

- I take time to go within and experience silence.

- I am grateful for being the person I am.

- I honor myself for all that I sacrificed.

- My boundaries provide a safety zone for me.

- My boundaries let others know how I expect to be treated.

- My boundaries help me form healthier relationships.

- I respect the boundaries of others as I do my own.

- I am proud of the woman that I am becoming.

- I have compassion for others because I have compassion for myself.

- I do not have to do anything to prove my worthiness.

- I belong here.

- I always win when I am being myself.

- I am good enough, just as I am.

- Who I am is becoming more with each day?

- Each day, I discover more about myself.

- My self-worth is unconditional.

- What I am feeling is valid, and it is part of my reality.

- I allow all of my feelings to present themselves without getting caught up in any of them.

- I am constantly growing and improving myself as a person.

- I let my feelings and energy guide me in life.

- I do not allow others to define me.

- The only person that I compare myself to is myself.

- I align myself to my life by trusting what feels right for me.

- I am deserving of self-care and self-love.

- I nurture myself so that I can nurture others.

- I honor my life, for it was bestowed on me for a reason.

- My life rejuvenates and restores itself when I give it attention.

- My body is beautiful and scared.

- I take care of myself because I am worth it.

- I am intentional in the way that I live.

- My privacy and alone time are sacred.

- I seek peace and simplicity.

- My growth and happiness are my responsibility.

- I am beneath no one, nor am I above anyone.

- I care for myself so that I can care for others.

- I am beautiful just as I am.

- I am beautiful and worthy of happiness.

- I am beautiful in my own right, as are others.

- I choose to be happy.

- I am whole; I have everything that I need to feel complete.

- I belong, and I have something to bring to the table

- I love my skin color.

- I love my hair.

- I honor my hopes and dreams.

- I make decisions that come from a place of love and caring.

- I have the right to say "no."

- I can say "no," without feeling guilty.

- I take my time to do things correctly instead of taking shortcuts.

- I do not feel self-pity, for I am a gift to others and myself.

- I love who I am, and I appreciate who I am.

- I do not need others to feel complete. I am complete as a person and enjoy and value my solitude.

- My past has no control over me.

- I love who I am, and I do not judge or criticize myself.

- I am happy being with me; I am comfortable in my own skin.

- Life loves me, and I love life.

- I am not beholden to anyone to warrant me sacrificing my happiness.

- I am learning to trust my decisions because I am learning to trust myself.

- I honor my body, for it is my temple to my creator.

- My mind and body were shaped and sculpted by my creator. My creator's hands carefully molded me to carry on his glorious work.

- I will not tolerate being judged for my skin color.

- I am growing as a person, and I have faith in my process.

- I will no longer compare myself to others.

- I celebrate my progress in becoming a better person.

- Every step forward that I take is deserving of my acknowledgment.

- I strive to always improve myself, yet, I will never reach perfection.

- I am ever-evolving in my knowledge, wisdom, and beauty.

- I have unconditional love for myself.

- I will not tolerate suggestions from others or myself that I am less than others.

- I do not need anyone's permission to do what I feel is right for me

- I am creative with great ideas.

- My presence in this world is meaningful as I make a difference simply by being me.

- My presence in this world is meaningful because I can make a difference.

- My presence in this world is meaningful because I care.

- I love my abilities and talents.

- I am patient with myself and give myself room to learn and grow.

- All the qualities I need to be happy and successful lie within me.

- I am good enough, capable enough, and worthy enough to succeed.

- I have intrinsic worth.

- I deserve the best, for I am worthy.

- Though others may not believe in asking for help, I do. It is my choice, and I deserve it.

- Though my family may not believe in seeking help for mental health concerns, I do. I deserve to be happy.

- My family may not believe in seeking help for health concerns, but I do. It is my choice, and it is my body.

- I am deserving of well-being, inner peace, and love. I deserve to be prosperous. I do not associate with anyone that believes otherwise.

- I look back to remind myself of all I had to overcome to be here today. In doing so, I celebrate my strength, determination, and resiliency.

- I speak from the heart.

- I am learning to love and appreciate myself.

- My compassion for others is growing.

- I have complete acceptance of my strengths and my weaknesses.

- I feel balanced and secure in my life.

- I remain centered as my emotions drift by like clouds.

- If I feel anxious around others, it is because I am receiving the message that I have forgotten the glory of who I am.

- Overcoming self-doubt takes time. I am loving and patient with myself, and I keep moving forward.

- I accept myself for who I am because that is the way to victory.

- Like the wings of a newly emerged butterfly, my flaws become my wings when they are brought to the sunlight of my acceptance.

- I am dragging my self-image out of the shadows of my judgments and presenting it to the light of self-love.

- I am worthy just as I as I am.

- I am enough because my creator made me who I am.

- My self-confidence is growing.

- I am confidently and courageously pursuing my dreams.

- I am complete as I am, and I am good enough.

- I am worthy of my boldest dreams, and I am worthy of manifesting them.

- I trust in my ability to succeed, and I believe in myself.

- Within me lies the power and great strength, and I am learning to express it.

- I do not let others' opinions of me shake my sense of dignity and self-worth.

- I accept that others may have opinions that clash with mine.

- I do not engage in spreading gossip or untruths about others.

- I am no less and no more deserving of good things than others.

- I am good enough and worthy enough.

- I am. Enough said.

- I accept that prejudice and sexism exist, but I will not hold on to hate or resentment.

- I provide support to others in a way that is consistent with my self-respect and dignity.

- I embrace my gifts, talents, and strengths.

- I can offer new perspectives and ideas that reflect my experience.

- I will use the perceptions that others have of me to empower me. I will never let the perceptions of others make me feel less.

- I let go of the need to impress others, for I have nothing to prove. I am perfect just as I am.

- I honor my need for rest and relaxation. I will honor myself by taking time daily for "me time."

- I love the way that I look. I love all of my features, including my imperfections.

- I offer value to people. I am a valuable resource for them.

- I enjoy showing others who I am and what I can offer.

- I take time for myself to relax and have a break. I treat self-care as a priority.

- I love myself, and I treat myself with respect. For this reason, I do not take on more than I can handle.

- I am comfortable saying "no" when it is necessary. My time is valuable, and I deserve to spend it as I choose.

- I bring a unique perspective to the table and my unique background.

- I am greeted by my creator's love every morning, and I am renewed.

- The strength and love of my creator reside within me at every moment.

- I am confident and strong.

- I am filled with the love and energy of the universe, and it renews me.

- I am proud of who I am.

- I am a gentle soul.

- I am a force for good.

- My feelings count.

- My life matters.

- I honor my feelings.

- I honor my beliefs.

- I am intelligent and wise.

- I am worthy of being where I am.

- I deserve everything that I have attained.

- I deserve to take care of myself because I work hard.

- I am good enough just as I am, yet, I strive to improve each day.

- I embrace my sexuality.

- I am forgiving and accepting of myself, and I move forward with my life.

- I am like a masterpiece. I am a classical work of art.

- I have no need to impress others as I have nothing to prove. I fully accept myself.

- I do not compare myself to others; I only judge myself by how far I have come in becoming a better version of myself.

- I am a strong and resilient woman.

- I choose to feel happy. I have the power to do so, and I have the right.

- I do not allow anyone in my life to disturb my sense of emotional well-being. I will replace them with those with who I share a connection.

- I affirm my humanity and allow myself to experience all of my emotions, make mistakes, fail, and succeed.

- I let go of my guilt, resentments, and hurts and opened myself to healing.

Final Words

One of the most important things to understand about attachment styles is that they are not some mental illness or disorder. They are learned ways of thinking and behaving, and we all have one. We can think of attachment styles as a language. We all grew up learning a certain language. Unless we have a secure attachment style, the language we grew up with no longer serves us.

We need to learn a new language to live a happier and more fulfilling life.

Using language as a metaphor for attachment styles is also valuable for my next point. Who you are as a person is not defined by the language you speak. Similarly, your attachment style does not define who you are either. You are not your attachment style. Rather, your attachment style shapes how you think and behave within certain moments of your relationships. I hope this book motivates you to make the necessary changes so that you may live the life you deserve.

BOOK #2

Crush Negative Thoughts

The Only Guide You Need to Break the
Negative Thought Patterns and Be Happy

Introduction

Overthinking is a silent crippler. It sneaks into your brain unnoticeably, and it latches and holds onto you for what feels like forever. So how does it even get in? Simply put, it starts because we worry about something. While that may be a gross oversimplification to some people, for this book, that will suffice as a general understanding of how it appears like you have become an overthinker seemingly overnight.

In truth, overthinking is often—but not always—latched onto a deeper mental condition such as depression, anxiety, eating disorders, or substance use disorders; but, that is not always the case. The problem is that the correlation between overthinking and those other conditions become a chicken and egg scenario. It is not entirely clear which came first and started the other until you deep dive with licensed professionals (Morin, 2020).

Just because overthinking is often linked to the above mental conditions does not mean that they always occur together; there are multiple other reasons that any of these conditions can occur, but it is good to mention them now, so that you can begin to create self-awareness.

Understanding Overthinking

The problem with overthinking is that because it is so prevalent in our lives, many people either dismiss their overthinking tendencies, or begin to develop an overthinking complex about overthinking. While this book is going to go more in-depth on how to identify your personal overthinking triggers and patterns, we are going to begin with a generalized understanding of overthinking and how it works.

What is Overthinking

The definition of overthinking is as follows: "To think too much about (something): to put too much time into thinking about or analyzing (something) in a way that is more harmful than helpful" (Merriam-Webster, n.d.). Before going any further into understanding overthinking, there is something very important in the definition which must be pointed out: Overthinking becomes dangerous when we think to the point that our thoughts become more harmful than helpful.

Another great way to look at it is to see that overthinking is very closely associated with worry or rumination; especially since those two actions can easily be justified as trying to do something beneficial or productive. For example, we explain to ourselves, friends, family members, and co-workers that we are worrying about someone's health, or that we are preparing ourselves for the worst outcome (Acosta, 2022). In actuality, we are mentally preparing for every worst-case scenario, and are really making things worse for ourselves in the long run.

By giving ourselves the conscious belief that we are doing something positive or productive through worrying, or engaging in ruminating thoughts, we allow those types of thoughts and behaviors to continue. The problem is that allowing ourselves to continue thinking this way actually encourages our brain to persist in the ingrained subconscious negative thinking patterns those types of thoughts induce.

Now, before going any further, we must acknowledge the elephant in the room. Yes, the above paragraphs make it seem like you, as an overthinker, are openly welcoming that type of thinking, into your mind with open arms. This book is not saying that. While you are technically in control over what thoughts you allow, overthinking is a habit, and it tends to begin associating anxious, obsessive, ruminative, depressive feelings—or any other type of associated negative feelings—to your original thoughts, without you even noticing. It is a sad fact, but most overthinkers are not even completely aware they overthink, or of the extent that their brain goes to while in that state. Which is why this book opened with the statement that overthinking is so pervasive and sneaky, and that most people perpetuate the cycle without even noticing it. If this is you, there is absolutely nothing to be ashamed of or upset over. A lot of us have engaged in over thinking at one point in time.

We all overthink sometimes. However, the key difference between an overthinker—where that type of thinking has become a way of life and way to create safety—compared to others, is what is done with the reasons behind overthinking. A non-overthinker will use specific scenarios where overthinking is necessary to create a positive outcome or to meet a requirement. Examples of this could be a project at work or finally coming up with a way to have a confrontation with someone close to them. However, overthinkers tend to use the exact same thought patterns to continue cycles of negativity, worrying, and self-loathing.

Essentially, if your overthinking phase has a pre-set end date (like a project due date or the day of that coffee with someone), and you are able to not overthink the scenario too much after the event then you are most likely not an overthinker. (It is completely normal, however, to go over a traumatic event for a few hours or days after the actual event, because you need time to process it.) True overthinkers fixate on anything and everything, and there really is no end date as to when that stops.

Why might that type of thinking have no end date? The answer to that could honestly be almost anything. It could be because your brain is wired this way (this will be discussed as we progress), it could be that something about your previous overthinking triggered something in your brain to keep it going, or it could be that the time you needed to overthink caused your brain to regress back to old ways of thinking. Sadly, overthinking is one of those things where it just pops up, and there could be many reasons as to why it has. Try to not let that dishearten you. While you may be an overthinker, or you may know someone who is, there are plenty of ways to fight it, and we will discuss many of those in this book. So, let's keep going.

How Overthinking Works

There are two main types of overthinking: worrying about the past, or worrying about the future (Morrin, 2019). Since these two ways of thinking are common in modern society, it makes sense that so many people ignore their overthinking tendencies. On top of that, the increased 'normal' levels of stress most of us now experience begin to alter our brains chemically, in the ways we think, and the actual size and abilities of our brains, which in turn enables overthinking to become a stronger habit (TED-Ed, 2015).

What Overthinking Is Not

Alright, so now that you have the definition of overthinking, and how it manifests, it is important that you understand what overthinking is *not.* Since overthinking latches onto thinking, is triggered by multiple unknown variables, and can even persist in your brain without your full awareness, let's just make sure that you fully understand what is happening, rather than worrying about every type of in-depth thinking we go through as humans. We are going to quickly run through a list of what overthinking is not, and why these types of thinking is not overthinking.

Problem Solving

Problem solving is an intensive form of thinking. It involves looking at every possible scenario to find the best solution and outcome. The main difference between problem solving and overthinking is that when you are problem solving, you are focused on finding a solution. In comparison, overthinking dwells on the problem, and never really finds a solution that is actually usable (Morrin, 2019).

Self-Reflection

While self-reflection can also cause negative mental spirals, the main difference between self-reflection and overthinking is that with healthy self-reflection, you are learning something about yourself (Morrin, 2019). In comparison, overthinking tends to dwell on anything and everything that is wrong with you, and will even come up with things that are not wrong, but that you now believe are wrong.

If that sounds a bit odd, think about a time when someone you know was down on themselves and believed something which was completely wrong about who and what they were, and what they could do. That right there is a form of overthinking. We somehow end up believing negative things about ourselves that no one else does.

Your Brain and Emotions

Okay, so now that overthinking has been given a good rudimentary understanding, it is time to look at your brain and emotions. Why? Because overthinking is emotionally based, and when our emotions are involved, it is helpful to understand the science behind them in order to completely understand what is happening to us

The Basics

As mentioned earlier, stress goes hand-in-hand with overthinking; and, it really does not matter where your stress comes from. Whether we overthink because we are stressed, or our stress comes from overthinking, it is still there. What stress does to your brain is particularly important to understand.

Now, before we make stress the ultimate villain, I need to be clear that it is not. Bursts of stress can be great for competitive or high-adrenaline events like sports, or help you possibly perform better at work or in school. The thing is, in order for that to happen, you have to be able to mentally handle your stress correctly. While this book will have a few ways on how to do that in an upcoming chapter, the ways we will discuss how to combat stress in this chapter will predominantly deal with overthinking rather than your overall life.

So, back to how stress impacts you. Chronic stress, such as constant arguments or a toxic work environment can actually affect the size, functionality, and even the most basic level of your genes within the brain. When your brain recognizes stress, it releases a chemical called cortisol, which gives your body that boost of energy to instantly take action in the situation. The problem is that high levels of cortisol over long periods of time will hurt your brain. It will stop your brain's fear center as well as the parts of your brain that help with learning, socializing, and controlling stress. Additionally, cortisol can cause your brain to shrink in size, specifically through a loss in brain synapses, and a reduction in these brain cells being made throughout the brain's regular functions (TED-Ed, 2015).

Overall, the constant presence of cortisol long term is very damaging, and opens your brain up to numerous potential problems such as anxiety and depression.

Going Deeper

So then, how does your brain affect your overthinking? Well, there are numerous ways it does that, but for the purposes of this book, we are going to focus mainly on the thoughts, rather than the chemical imbalances.

Thanks to Dr. Carolyn Leaf and her peers, this topic has begun to be broken down into more easily understandable pieces, the first of which is that your brain and your mind are actually two completely separate entities residing in the same 'area' (your brain). Our thoughts are the very first thing that happens before anything else, and they occur in our minds. If we want to change, we have to change our thoughts. Think about it. If you want to lose weight, you have to actually come up with that thought in your mind. Our minds are where we react and respond to life around us. Since our mind is separate from our brain, what our mind decides directly influences our brain and how it functions.

Your mind thinks, and your brain reacts and responds.

's vs **Memories**

⸺ur thoughts are the product of how our minds respond to our lives while we are asleep. Our thoughts are actual physical things inside of our brains. If you ever remember seeing tree-like structures when discussing brains and neural pathways, thoughts are those trees. They are your thoughts, and the emotions tied to them. Consider a tree and what it is made of. Our memories are the roots of the trees inside our brains. Our thoughts themselves are what created that tree, and as the moment passes, the tree becomes inhabited by a memory of that thought. Every one of these thought trees can have hundreds of memories inside of them. What is that tree rooted to? Your brain. Which means that you are literally building into your brain the responses of your mind which come from your experiences, words, feelings, choices, and responses. This is how we begin to function, create good memories, and also how we create trauma within our brains.

A thought is made up of memories. Think of a photo album. The thought is the event being photographed, and the memories are the photographs.

All right, this is now the incredibly important bit for this book: The events in our environment are neurally encoded into our brains and bodies, and we know this thanks to psychoneurobiology. Therefore, whatever we constantly think about creates a stronger encoding on that particular thought and its associated emotions. In simpler terms, whatever we think about the most, grows. And as many of us know, what we think, feel, and choose, begins to dictate what we say, do, and even how we approach life. Therefore, when we constantly think about negative things, or think using negative thought patterns—like overthinking—we are building negativity into our brains (Leaf, 2019).

Breathe

Alright, that was a lot to get through, and a lot of very big facts thrown your way. Since this book is about overthinking, that was potentially a lot of new information to give your most-likely cortisol-happy brain to now begin turning over repeatedly.

First: Just because this is what is happening when you are overthinking does not mean this is what is happening now, or that your brain is always this way. The previous section merely mentions what happens when your brain is exposed to too much cortisol over long periods of time.

Second: Your brain is able to bounce back. Thanks to numerous wonderful studies and professionals who have done quite a bit of research, we know that when you put in the hard work, your brain is able to heal and fix itself (TEDx Talks, 2020a). However, it should be noted that while our brains can change and adapt, there also comes a very strong argument on the type of environment you are constantly putting your brain into. Your brain is adaptable and is wired for change, but it cannot change when it is fighting every type of environmental factor possible (there are maybe a few people among thousands of others who have this mental strength). Therefore, start to be mindful of the environments you are putting yourself into. If your surrounding environment is always negative, you are going to have a very hard time remaining and staying positive (TEDx Talks, 2020b). If you want your brain to overcome overthinking and adapt to a new normal, then you are going to have to begin to set yourself up for success.

Before Continuing

Before going further into overthinking, there are a few other things you should know and do while reading this book. It is heavily advised that you read and consider these things before continuing.

Terms

Some terms in this book may not be familiar to a few of you. In case that happens, they will be explained in this section. Many of these terms and ideas can be used in areas of your life outside of overthinking, so if you see something that you can use in another area, go ahead and do that!

Safe People

Safe people are the people in our lives who we can tell absolutely anything to and they will never judge us, harm us, or guilt us into changing our mind. They may encourage us to make better or different choices, but they respect us as a human and foster personal, professional, and relational growth (Cloud & John Sims Townsend, 2022/2016). These are the types of people who will never judge us and it is one of the healthiest relationships you have.

It is strongly recommended that for certain aspects of this journey, you ask one of your safe people to come alongside you and help you work through certain things. A bonus of using a safe person over a licensed therapist is that they have most likely known you a long time, and can add clarity and insight where your memories are not exactly the most reliable.

There will be many times in this book where your safe people will be mentioned, and you may even be encouraged to talk to them. However, be sure to make your safe person aware of what they are agreeing to. It is not fair, or necessarily kind, to make your safe person an accountability partner, or to bring them on this journey if they are unaware of that. Additionally, it would cause them to not give you the best advice.

If You Do Not Have a Safe Person

Sadly, there are times in our lives where safe people are not easily accessible, or those relationships are no longer as strong as they once were. If that is the case, find a professional therapist or licensed counselor for those times when you need help. These are the only type of people who can be safe right away, because they are professionally trained and most likely have quite a few other clients with similar problems.

Do not make someone you just met a safe person. While there is the potential for that down the road, the reason safe people are safe is because you have spent time getting to know them and building that relationship. Additionally, a new person may not be aware of how much you overthink, and what is more, they may not know enough of you as a person and your personal history to give you the best advice.

Accountability Partner

Similar to safe people, accountability partners are people who hold us accountable for certain things in our lives. This can be to stop us from continuing a negative pattern or to help us through an addiction. For this book, accountability partners will be used as a safeguard to ensure that you begin implementing the steps needed to stop overthinking; or, to encourage you as you scale up some of the practices you pick from this book.

When picking an accountability partner, you need to find someone you will listen to. Someone who can get into your face, get in touch with you to check up on you, and who you trust. You will also need to be prepared for what your accountability partner brings to the table. You need to be okay with the fact that they will get in your face, call you out, and ask for updates. You will also need to be honest with them. Lying to an accountability partner is like wearing a snowsuit in the desert it will do you absolutely no good. If your accountability partner makes you feel less than, or you do not feel comfortable sharing your failures with them because of their behaviors or reactions, find a different accountability partner.

Additionally, just like with safe people, these people need to be aware that they are your accountability partner so that they can fulfill that role. An accountability partner who is unaware that that is their role will do you no good in ensuring you are maintaining the steps for the habits when things get hard, or when you have a bad day.

Boundaries

According to Dr. Henry Cloud, boundaries are recognizing what we are, or are not, willing to be responsible for in our own lives (Cloud & John Sims Townsend, 2022/2004). This is especially important in overthinking, as it is beginning to build the mental and emotional awareness of when your thoughts are beginning to put more responsibility on you than you need, or should be accountable for in that particular scenario.

When you are having trouble thinking about if something is actually your responsibility, begin to relate that situation to an item of clothing, or to your house. We all know what we are or are not responsible for when it comes to material things. For instance, think about homeowners. Homeowners are very well-versed on what is their responsibility compared to other people such as their neighbors or municipal governments; and they have the tendency to not bend on those responsibilities. Similarly, most people are perfectly aware of what they own or want to add to their closet. Simply begin to ask yourself what you are willing to be and should be responsible for here in a given situation. If you need another incentive to start setting boundaries for yourself, knowing your boundaries is a great way to begin combatting overthinking, because it forces your brain and emotions to recognize what is your problem, and what is not.

Small Note

The 'should' in that above statement is in regards to personal responsibilities, and not what someone else is putting onto you. For instance, if you are responsible for managing the team meetings at work, your boundary cannot directly go against that (unless there is a dangerous and unhealthy situation), because that is what you agreed to when you took on that position (if it is not, then you should talk to your boss). In comparison, say your partner or friend is mad that you went to a different restaurant than what they wanted, but they did not speak up about their preference, when asked.

Between the two examples, one is clearly showing a responsibility that you have whether you want it or not, versus a situation where someone put a responsibility onto you that was never yours to begin with (to read their mind and know which restaurant they wanted to go to). Overthinking tends to fall into the second category, except you are the one who puts more of the responsibility onto yourself. Beginning to recognize when you do that will be incredibly beneficial throughout the rest of this book.

Toxic Positivity

Toxic positivity is a bit of a new term, which can sadly be overgeneralized to the point where it sounds like being positive is toxic. That is not what this term means. Toxic positivity is essentially the act of belittling your emotions or a negative scenario in order to remain positive. It is all well and good to use positivity to cheer yourself or others up, but it should not be done at the cost of someone's emotions or neglecting to honor their scenarios (Cherry, 2021).

There are tons of great resources and examples of showing the difference between toxic positivity and actually encouraging and helping someone, but for now, we will go through one brief example. For instance, instead of generalizing and saying, "It will be fine," you can specifically ask, "How can I help you?" In this example, the sentiments are the same, since the first one was most likely said with the underlying intent of trying to cheer someone up and be helpful, but the second example explicitly acknowledges that the person you are talking to needs help and you are willing to provide some.

It may seem small and trivial, but directly acknowledging someone's pain and problems—even though it may feel awkward—sometimes be all the person needs. Especially in regards to overthinking. As overthinkers, we tend to overgeneralize and belittle our own feelings and emotions—or over exaggerate them—to the point where we know we need help, but are unwilling to ask. Then, when faced with toxic positivity in the form where we actually feel like our feelings are being ignored, we shut down and do not attempt to continue asking for help.

Journaling

Journaling, whether it be on a notepad, document, or recorded voice memo, is a great way to begin gaining perspective on things you notice, are concerned about, or even just beginning to recognize as important self-reflection moments. This habit will also be incredibly beneficial while reading this book, as it will help you begin to gain perspective and really narrow down your overthinking habits and what you personally will need to focus on.

The chapters within this book will each have a journaling section where you will be encouraged to begin thinking about what you have read and how it directly correlates to you. When you are answering and thinking about these questions, there are several things you need to remember. First, these journals are meant to be the big picture of your life, its events, and your thoughts, feelings, and introspections. Meaning, it is completely okay to go on a long tangent and forget what you were saying, or to bring up an old painful memory. Sometimes, spilling our hearts out onto a piece of paper, including those weird mental tangents, helps bring us a clarity we would never achieve otherwise. So go for it. Second, these journaling moments are going to bring out many introspective moments. Meaning, you are going to have to take long and hard looks at your own emotions and the 'why' behind them. You may not always fully get the 'why,' but even beginning to think that way will help you begin to get to the point of where and how overthinking rooted itself into your daily life.

Be Honest

When it comes to overthinking, we may not always be sure what is the actual truth, since our brains have most likely muddled everything to the point where nothing is clear, and we feel like we are floating above ground. When it comes to journaling, or any other part of this process, you need to be honest with yourself about where you are in your overthinking process. Lying to yourself, ignoring warning signs in your brain, or pushing through those feelings, will not be helpful. There is a difference between perseverance and ignoring a clear warning sign. Remember, no one has to see this journal, and no one really should (unless you want to share it). So let the ugly truth out, because if you are not honest even in your own journal, you are never going to be honest with yourself, and a lot of the prompts and helpful ideas and suggestions in this book will be of no help. This includes allowing yourself to feel and express certain emotions, even if you know they are disproportionate to the scenario or that you cannot fully understand why you are feeling a certain way.

It may take awhile for you to begin differentiating between these things while overthinking in the beginning. Be honest about even that. If you are not honest to yourself about this journey, then you are allowing another loophole to exist that your overthinking brain might take advantage of.

While it is painful, messy, and sometimes brings up things we wish we did not have to admit about ourselves, honesty and determination are the key to change. You already have the determination, because you are reading this book. It is the honesty bit that may be a bit more challenging, but you can do it.

Be Human

It might sound strange, but prepare yourself to be okay being human. This means that certain portions of this book may be messy, will not be fun, and you may encounter parts of yourself or ways of thinking that you do not like. You do not have to like any of it, but you do have to embrace it and use those traits to propel yourself forward. Allowing yourself to be human will hopefully be the open door you need to begin encouraging that mindset and concession in regards to the standards you normally hold yourself to.

This Will Be a Journey

While it may not need to be said, since this book is about overthinking, it is worth the gamble to remind you: This journey will be worth it, and you are not alone. Overthinking is sadly quite common, especially in younger generations. Do not let the overthinking and negative mental pathways convince you that you are alone. You are not. You can do this, and you are completely able to do this. You may not succeed right away, and you may need to try and restart several times. But the journey will be worth it.

Get Help

Do not be afraid to get professional help if you think you need it. There is nothing to be ashamed of in admitting that you need someone who can constantly be in your life to help you, and paying a licensed therapist or counselor is a safe way to do it.

Whatever way you decide to continue on this journey, there is no shame in what you did, and you can change it to meet your needs.

Chapter 1

Overthinking Is the Root of It All

This may sound almost too simplistic for how intensive this book is about to become (if it has not hit that point already), but overthinking is most likely the root of many problems in your life. Even ones you have not considered yet.

For instance, have your friends and family, or partner, been saying that you are not being present, or you have been putting off having discussions with them? Have you been meaning to do certain things—which really should not take long for you to do—but they seem to never get done?

There are plenty of small, seemingly harmless examples like those above which may actually be a product of you overthinking; a form of paralysis. (Or, you could just be a procrastinator, or have many other logical reasons as to why those things have not happened.)

However, you did buy this book.

In case you are unsure, or you want concrete examples of what overthinking might look like, this chapter will cover exactly that. We will go through what thinking about thinking is, how it relates to overthinking, and then begin to go through several symptoms and causes of being an overthinker.

Thinking About Thinking

It may sound a bit odd, but thinking about thinking is a great way to know if you are an overthinker. Let's break that down a bit. When it comes to overthinking, thinking about thinking looks like you are obsessing and overanalyzing your thoughts constantly. It might even be at the point where you are doing this subconsciously in non-stressful situations. It has become a habit. One that is actually quite exhausting and not at all good for your brain, your emotions, or you in the long run.

What's worse, thinking about thinking could look harmless or even be guised as being productive, because you are thinking about your thoughts and how you are going about those thoughts. Yet the main difference between an overthinker who is thinking about thinking, and someone who is actually attempting to build more awareness about their thoughts, is what they do with it (which is going to become a common trend in comparing overthinkers to non-overthinkers). For instance, an overthinker will use thinking about thinking to continue a negative cycle and begin to actually create obsessive thoughts about their thinking. In comparison, a non-overthinker who is thinking about thinking is consciously being aware of their thoughts to be able to change habits they have accidentally created.

Consider the following example:

Amy is having a stressful day at work and ended up having a pretty heated conversation with her friend, Anne. While the conflict was resolved, Amy began to replay that conversation over and over in her head throughout the rest of the week, and began to doubt her choices, words, and even her friendship with Anne, even though they had resolved the conflict the same day.

In comparison, Anne took a look at her conflict with Amy and began to break down their conversation to see where she could have handled things better. Anne was able to responsibly admit what was her fault, what she could have done better, and what was not her fault in the entire scenario. Anne began to identify and think about where she could improve her interpersonal skills and started to create habits to change those reactions for future conflicts.

Amy used her thinking about thinking to begin a negative cycle about herself and her relationship, which in turn, contributed to her overthinking habit. In comparison, Anne used thinking about thinking to bring hindsight and clarity to where she could improve her relationship with Amy going forward.

What Anne did in the example is called 'metacognition,' which is the art of regulating and changing your thoughts and actions to consciously create a form of heightened self-awareness. While metacognition is actually one of the end-goals of this book, it is not what overthinkers generally gravitate towards while overthinking. Overthinkers use thinking about thinking to constantly obsess and over analyze their thoughts and actions to the point where they begin to create self-doubt, worry, anxiety, and maybe even depression.

If you do this, do not worry. We will go over other signs and manifestations of overthinking, but bringing up thinking about thinking was really the hook to get some of you who were unsure about whether you were actually an overthinker or not to begin questioning some of your mental habits and responses.

Signs You Are an Overthinker

In this section, we will discuss the signs of an overthinker as well as give examples on how these types of thinking and actions can present themselves. Each section will also contain examples of non-overthinkers, to help gain perspective on where overthinking begins to take over a relatively normal way of thinking.

Obsessive and Anxious Thoughts

When you are in a stressful situation, like a work project, deciding to end a relationship, or preparing for a confrontation with someone close to you, it is perfectly normal, natural, and healthy to obsess and be anxious over it—as long as those thoughts are within the immediate lead-up and aftermath of that particular scenario.

Why is this healthy? Because first of all it is for a short period of time. The before and after, if you will. During those times you are preparing yourself and then de-escalating your after-rush of endorphins in direct response to a relatively traumatic or stressful situation. Whether you actually are or not, your brain is mentally preparing you to go to war. You need all those hyped-up emotions to get through it and survive after the event.

The problem is when these obsessive and anxious thoughts are in no way related to an immediate trigger for stress. Perhaps you constantly go over one particular conversation or scenario, or perhaps you are always anxious about what could happen, what people think, or what you have done. Another way to look at it is if you are constantly worrying.

Worrying in and of itself is a relatively common enough mental state, unfortunately; however, there is a time and place to worry. For example, if you are in the hospital or you are going into a serious meeting. Those are definitely times in your life when you should worry. Even low-key worrying about if your partner's parents will like you, or even just meeting someone new in general, is normal and natural.

Being obsessive and anxious about your thoughts and worries, however, is not. What makes it worse is that oftentimes we use these worry cycles and obsessive and anxious thoughts as a mental 'relief.' We believe that if we think about these things enough, we will be able to prepare ourselves for what is to come, and in turn, somehow magically prevent our worrying and anxiety about the uncertain future (Stein, n.d.). The problem is that the solution our brains have come up with actually encourages the types of thoughts which make our worries worse.

That may have been a little confusing. Consider this example:

June constantly worries about her future. To prepare for it, she constantly thinks about it. Specifically, she thinks about how her day will go, what kinds of interactions she will have with her co-workers, and how the dinner with her family will go. Except, instead of thinking about her general, pretty easy-going life, June constantly mentally imagines arguments with her friends, family, and co-workers, to 'better prepare' herself for when those confrontations come.

Now, it is all well and good to prepare yourself for a confrontation when you know—or assume—one is going to happen. If you know that your boss is going to have a serious chat with you, hyping yourself up or going over your past work projects to be prepared is normal and expected. If you believe you are going to have an uncomfortable talk with your parents, mentally going over what they may say and how you will defend yourself, is normal. Notice how each of these things are in the immediate build-up? June's example did not have that build-up. It was her daily mentality.

This type of thinking is exhausting, and it encourages your brain to build negative thought patterns around conflict and other areas of your life. Remember the introduction and that segment about your brain? The more you think about something, the stronger those thoughts and memories will be in your mind, making those brain chemical reactions stronger in your body.

This is all well and good when these are happy or good emotional responses to healthy situations, but when it is about situations which have not come to pass, we are beginning to waste a lot of mental energy on things that do not deserve that much mental output. Additionally, we are not really preparing ourselves for anything. We are not even stopping the worry that we originally wanted to fix.

Reminder

If you connected with any of what was said above, remember to breathe. It is okay if this happens to you. The first step is awareness, and now you have that.

Take a moment if you need to, and let's keep going.

Painful Rumination

There are always going to be those times when we remember that painfully embarrassing moment in our pre-teen, teen, or young adult years where we consciously made a decision, which in hindsight, was maybe not the best thing to do. However, in non-overthinking brains, these types of instances are very occasional, and are often remembered with a small wince and the ability to move past that particular occasion.

Overthinkers, on the other hand, painfully rethink and relive multiple moments in their lives, which honestly may not even be worthy of that much memory. However, by that point, their brain has made this type of thinking a habit, and they may not even be consciously aware of what they are doing. On top of that, they painfully ruminate, which means they re-think their thoughts repetitively over every single aspect of the situation using emotions like regret, self-loathing, and self-blame (Welle (www.dw.com), 2020).

Overthinkers constantly do this. They constantly remind themselves of painful memories and continue to overanalyze scenarios which are no longer in their control, and have no possibility to be solved. Now, there is a clear line between looking at a recent scenario in hindsight and admitting where you could have done better, versus painfully ruminating over something.

For instance, say you recently went through a breakup. Many people will agree there is a reasonable length of time where it is socially acceptable to admit your own fault in the breakup. Saying things like, "Well, that was my mistake," or "In hindsight, I could have done this better," and then using those reflections to better prepare yourself for your next relationship, is in no way painfully ruminating over the breakup. However, if you are reflecting on a breakup with thoughts like, "I should have been more supportive," "I have lost my soulmate," or "I am unlovable," then those thoughts are sadly one hundred percent painful rumination and overthinking behaviors (Welle (www.dw.com), 2020).

The Difference

If you are still unsure, let's examine the two examples more closely. The first instance admits where they had done wrong, but does not make the other person an angel in the relationship. Instead, they clearly defined boundaries around what they did wrong, and what they could change in themselves.

In comparison, the second person does not even focus on bettering themselves at all, but rather on how unattractive physically and emotionally they are now that they no longer have a partner.

A great antidote for it, as perfectly described by a friend is, "Going to the garden to eat worms." Sometimes, overthinkers become so caught up in the negative cycle of their own thoughts that they begin to spiral to the point where they feel unloved, unworthy, and that they may as well go sit in the garden and eat worms, because no one will stop them or even care enough to stop them. This type of thinking is a result of painful rumination, because we, as overthinkers, painfully ruminate over self-deprecating thoughts to the point where we believe them.

Again, if this is you, do not be ashamed. You are worthy of love, affection, and someone wanting the best for you. You are worthy of wanting the best and getting the best. Do not let the painful rumination win, it is a struggling uphill battle, but together we can do it.

Perfectionism

Perfectionism is something many of us unconsciously strive for. We want to be perfect in that hobby, we want to be perfect for our partner, etc. It may not even seem like perfection to you. It could simply be labeled as wanting to be your 'best.' And best is okay, because the word and colloquialism for that saying generally means that your best changes with you. For example, say you begin to take up running. Giving and doing your best in the beginning may be a short distance, or shorter intervals of running at a time. Yet, as you progress in your running journey, so will your ability to go longer in distance and without breaks, making your best grow with your body.

Perfectionism, on the other hand, does not grow with you. It limits you. At its very core, perfectionism is the need to be or appear perfect, or to believe that perfection is even possible to achieve. When it comes to perfection in relation to overthinking, there are two main problems. The first is that many people believe that there is such a thing as 'healthy perfectionism' to justify this type of behavior. Except, a better way to describe 'healthy perfectionism' is what was just discussed: trying for our best. In comparison between perfectionism and trying your best, the most distinctive difference is that when you try your best you are willing to admit your best may not be perfect, and that you are opening yourself to failure. This type of vulnerability is hard for anyone, but when you pair it with overthinkers the vulnerability which is required when trying your best becomes almost paralyzing, as it is forcing your brain to begin considering how you might fail.

Which brings up the second problem. Opening yourself up to failure—meaning you are letting yourself be vulnerable—is removing the shield perfectionism provides (Good Therapy, 2019). Sounds odd, right? Think about it. As an overthinker, your brain is fighting multiple things at once. You are fighting your own feelings of inadequacy, plus possibly years of training your brain to think negatively about yourself, while also attempting to be vulnerable enough to admit your failures to yourself and potentially others. Which then makes the shield of perfectionism seem much more safe and easy, because you are still putting in the work—or at least, you think you are—to improve yourself without potentially making a fool of yourself at the same time.

The problem is that perfectionism is almost impossible to maintain constantly, and is definitely exhausting to emulate. Additionally, perfectionism brings with itself a whole new set of problems which latch onto overthinking, such as analysis paralysis and information overload.

How does it do that?

Well, first of all, perfectionism, analysis paralysis, and information overload all stem from the constant thought that we are not good enough. We are not good enough at this hobby, we are not getting better quickly enough, etc., and if we have this innate belief that we must be perfect, then we will of course develop a type of paralysis when we know we cannot achieve that perfectionism immediately. Our brains are too busy thinking about how we can get there and how we can make the physical actions of what we are thinking about be the most perfect the first time around. Additionally, our brain becomes overloaded from all of the information we have shoved into it to try and process the scenario, while simultaneously figuring out how we can be perfect at it our first go-round.

Then, let's not forget the paralysis that comes with this type of thinking. Everything that has been described so far sounds pretty overwhelming. Which is exactly what happens. Your brain is so full with every possible scenario, your fears, your desires, and its inability to think in a new way (due to your overthinking patterns and habits) that it begins to get paralyzed and shut down. What this feels like is when you suddenly freeze or cannot make a decision because you just cannot seem to legitimately think of one.

While those are what happens in an overthinking brain, non-overthinking brains do experience events where they also desire to be perfect. A great example is the term 'bridezilla,' If you are unsure what that term means, it is used to describe a woman who is normally quite reasonable but has become an absolute monster in regards to her wedding. Everything has to be just so, and everything has to be perfect. Even though this example is incredibly specific, it points out how there are certain times when perfectionism is not related to overthinking, but is rather a one-off want or desire motivated by something else entirely. It may still not be incredibly healthy, but if your perfectionism is related to a one-off scenario which will not be repeated, or you do not repeat that need for perfectionism for every one-off scenario, then your overthinking most likely does not manifest in the form of perfectionism.

Similarly, everyone experiences brain paralysis at some point in time, and probably multiple times. Adrenaline athletes experience it almost regularly, as their brain cannot catch up to what their bodies are doing, and they have to rely on instinct and ingrained decision making to ensure that their body does what is necessary in that situation. However, overthinkers tend to experience this kind of paralysis almost daily, and not even in adrenaline-infused situations.

Why?

Because their brain is so busy coming up with ways to ensure that the innate desire for perfection is maintained, while also analyzing every possible bit of information given (along with mental scenarios and play-alongs).

Again, these are all signs of being an overthinker, but you do not have to have all of them. You may experience a combination of them, or some of them may only become apparent in relevant situations. The point is, you are an overthinker because you are literally overthinking everything, including whether you are an overthinker or not.

So, in summary, the cycle goes like this: As an overthinker, you latch onto perfectionism because you do not want to be vulnerable to other people in whatever hobby or scenario it is (or perhaps it is everywhere in your life). Then, because you are trying too hard to be perfect, you begin to develop an information overload on how to maintain that perfection during your action, which then brings up analysis paralysis, because your brain is too busy trying to process all of the information and analyze which is your best bet to get the perfection you want.

Obsession

As has been hinted at in other sections, overthinking has a strong correlation to obsession. When we overthink we tend to begin obsessing over our thoughts. This could be where we went wrong, how we can hide our imperfections, how we can stay perfect, etc. No matter what the actual thought is, it is normally a negative one, which honestly is not the best thing to be obsessing over.

Before getting too offended or upset, it is also reasonably associated that by this point the obsessive thoughts are more so a habit or subconscious thought, which is then brought into the conscious, rather than an active decision. Once your brain is accustomed to making certain types of associations, it will begin automatically making those associations whether we want it to or not; including obsessing over whatever has popped into our mind.

The problem is that for overthinkers, this means that their brain begins to get accustomed to wasting lots of mental energy obsessing over thoughts which do not need to be re-examined. While it sounds harsh, it is true. Going over a negative scenario or thought briefly and succinctly to analyze and make better choices is a great way to learn and begin to emulate self-regulating behaviors. However, overthinkers do not do it briefly, succinctly, or with the goal of actually bettering themselves. Oh, you may have that intent and that may be what you are telling yourself when you go over a scenario for the hundredth time. However, start to ask yourself this question: Is going over this scenario really going to help me be better, or am I using this as an excuse to focus on everything negative in my life and about me?

If your answer is 'yes' to that question, do not lose heart, because you are now aware of what you are doing and why. Take a moment and breathe, because at one point, we have all been there. Even non-overthinkers have moments or phases where they have used something guised as healthy behavior to enable unhealthy habits. The thing is, now that you are aware, you can stop it.

In general, obsession is something which can be either good or bad; it depends on the obsession and how it affects your life. Even being obsessed with physical fitness to the point where you ignore the rest of your life and responsibilities is unhealthy. The same can be said for obsessive thoughts. Sometimes being captivated by a type or way of thinking is normal. Yet, overthinkers use obsessive thoughts to constantly think about the negatives in their life and exemplify every other type of thought which has been discussed so far.

Always Questioning

As you have probably guessed, always questioning does help sometimes when it is a positive way to think or be. For instance, like when you are working on a work project, trying to figure out what clients want, or wanting any type of clarification for immediate situations. The problem with overthinkers is that this constant questioning is not just in positive and required areas. They will always question themselves, and those around them, beyond figuring out what is needed in the moment. A great example would be always asking your partner if they truly love you, or questioning why your parents are willing to help you.

Questioning acts of love, or even basic societal niceties, is a sign of overthinking, because you are questioning things that have given no indication that that type of question is necessary. In general, non-overthinkers do not question if these acts of love, service, or social niceties are deserved or question if they have earned them. Overthinkers, on the other hand, often do. That is not okay because it is putting you in a constant stressful situation. Do not worry, though; we will continue to fight this together and give you ways to begin reframing those questions into healthy and positive ways of thinking.

Stop

Now, there is a good chance that if you are an overthinker, you are suddenly overthinking everything you have read so far and are perhaps questioning yourself, your reality, your thoughts, and maybe even your intentions.

If you are doing that, take a moment to breathe.

Remember, this chapter is to help you affirm that you are overthinking and begin to set the groundwork for noticing when and how you overthink.

Self-Doubt

Ah, self-doubt. This type of thinking is pervasive and can be considered the root for many other forms of thinking which have been discussed so far. So what is it? While it is pretty self-explanatory, just in case this is a term which is unfamiliar to you (which is completely okay), self-doubt is, well, doubting yourself. In regards to overthinking, this type of doubting goes so far as to cause you to begin questioning things you know you can do, to the point where you become self-critical and self-destructive.

In some circumstances, such as a new job, new hobby, or new relationship, doubting yourself and your abilities is a natural and normal response. However, in healthy scenarios, your personal growth and problem-solving skills allow you to proactively fight any self-doubts which occur. For instance, say that you are doubting whether you will be able to maintain a new job. However, you fight through those doubts and over time begin to overcome them, because you are able to identify your problem areas and proactively confront them. In comparison, overthinkers use their self-doubt as a way to begin cycling into their predominant thought patterns where, instead of looking for proactive solutions to prove they can do something, they get overwhelmed and defeated by their self-doubt, to the point where they are unable to see past their own mental cycles.

Yet, when it comes to overthinkers, self-doubt is incredibly pervasive and hard to identify in some cases, as well as fight. This is mainly because self-doubt so easily attaches itself to other forms of overthinking, such as perfectionism and painful rumination. Self-doubt can be viewed as a gateway into the other forms of overthinking, because the feeling of self-doubt can so easily lead to everything else which has been discussed so far. On closer consideration, it makes sense.

Since the very essence of self-doubt is doubting yourself to the point where you freeze and forget how to do something, even if you know you can do it, your brain is then able to introduce other negative thought patterns on top of those doubts. Why? Because your brain is so used to thinking in negative cycles. If your brain is already accustomed to being negative, and it has gotten to the point where it—and yourself—are disbelieving of being capable of doing anything positive, then it makes sense that the 'next best thing' would be to latch onto negative thought patterns.

Compared to the other forms of overthinking, self-doubt is probably one of the strongest forms used by overthinkers, because it is often used as a reason to not continue on bettering yourself, for the reasons mentioned above.

Post-Read Breathe

This chapter and previous segments were a lot to take in. So now it is time to take a breath. If you have begun to notice some ways that you think align with this section, that is okay. Identifying where you are overthinking and wasting mental energy does not mean you are a failure, it does not mean something is wrong with you, and it does not mean that you are incapable of fixing this if you want to. Awareness is the first step, and this chapter was written with the intent of causing you to raise awareness within and about yourself.

What it does mean is that you will have to start building strong forms of mental self-awareness, which we will discuss in a later chapter.

Now, for the small number of you who may be reading this to try and gain understanding for a loved one who is an overthinker, or to see if this book would be helpful for an overthinker, do not let this chapter get to you. As has been said numerous times, there are plenty of situations where each of these signs are healthy reactions in occasional instances. The key word here is 'occasional.' It is perfectly normal to feel self-doubt when starting a new job in a completely new career. It is one hundred percent okay to be in pain over an old awkward memory from when you were a pre-teen. Those types of thoughts—if they are few and far between—happen to us all, whether we are overthinkers or not.

However, if it is happening frequently, and more than you would like to admit. It is time to do some deep hard-truth diving into yourself.

Journaling

So, with all of this information in mind, it is time to begin journaling some thoughts, questions, and answers. For these journaling sections, please, be honest with yourself. No one has to see this journal. No one has to know. But it is best to be honest on paper because then at least somewhere on this Earth, you have made the conscious decision to be truthful to yourself.

Take a moment and if you have to re-read parts of this chapter, make sure you do that. But for now, start to think about how you personally overthink. Is there one way in particular that you use, or is it a combination of all of them? Is there a particular trigger that you are aware of for these thoughts, or perhaps for even certain types of these thoughts?

A few great questions to get the ball rolling, and to start your introspective journey, is to ask yourself the following questions:

- Do you overthink?

- Do you think about thinking?

- Do you catch yourself obsessing over past thoughts or interactions with other people and obsessing about it to the point where you now have raised anxiety?

Chapter 2

The Obsessions And Anxieties Of An Overthinker

Even though the last chapter specifically discussed obsession and anxiety in relation to overthinking, those examples and discussions tended to either give one specific example, or were written with the intent of giving you a good base of understanding for how obsession and anxiety worked with overthinking.

In this chapter, we are going to go into specific types of obsessions and anxieties, specifically in regards to how it is affecting your life through four main areas: habits, relationships, your job, and physical activity and miscellaneous circumstances. To give you as best of an understanding on how obsession and anxiety works with overthinking, this chapter will be divided into three sections. The first two sections will discuss obsessions and anxieties in relation to an overthinking as well as non-overthinking brain, to help you begin to notice when thoughts are related to overthinking, versus a naturally-triggered response to certain situations you might find yourself in. The third section will discuss how obsession and anxieties in relation to overthinking—as well as overthinking in and of itself—may be present within your own life. This section will also include examples and a step-by-step guide to show where the overthinking begins.

Please note, these examples are simply examples. They are meant to be used as a guide for you to begin your journey to awareness and to begin monitoring and noticing certain thought patterns which may be occurring in your own brain.

So, without further ado, let's begin.

Obsessions

According to Merriam-Webster, an obsession is "a persistent disturbing preoccupation with an often unreasonable idea or feeling," or, "broadly: compelling motivation" (Merriam-Webster, n.d.-a). Before diving into the overthinkers and how they tend to obsess, it should first be noted that there is a term going around colloquially called 'healthy obsession.' Essentially, this definition is based on the broad definition of obsession, and is used to bring a new twist on how to implement healthy habits into your life. People who use obsession in a healthy way essentially use the terminology to begin motivating themselves to engage in more healthy habits.

However, when it comes to overthinking, obsession tends to present itself in a more negative light; predominantly through two 'different' ways. (For the purposes of this book, we are going to say two ways, but they are closely interlinked and could arguably be seen as extensions of each other.)

The first way is a form of avoidance, or a way to 'heal' past traumas. Oddly enough, obsession becomes almost like a mental Band-Aid for a past problem which overthinkers cannot resolve, for whatever reason. These reasons could be past traumas, the inability or lack of desire to dig deeper, or perhaps even the inability to continue on their healing journey due to a mental roadblock, confusion on where to go, or the sad fact of being in the middle of doing the grunt work for fixing their mental pathways and how they think. Regardless as to why it has happened, to some overthinkers, obsessing over certain scenarios, relationships, or even the potential 'what ifs' in our lives becomes the magic elixir which will fix all their problems. Which in itself is problematic, because they are not using their obsessive thoughts in a positive way to actually bring about healing and change. This then brings up the second way that obsession can be used by overthinkers: as a form of continuing the worry or negativity cycle.

Let's be honest. We have all been there. We have all experienced days, weeks, perhaps even months or years where everything is constantly going wrong and we see no end in sight to the misery. Maintaining a positive, or even pragmatic, mindset during those times is understandably difficult . Now, take those types of thoughts and feelings of it never getting better, and you begin to get a tiny glimpse into an overthinker's head when it comes to using obsessive thoughts to continue their personal worry or negativity cycle. As mentioned in the previous chapter, these types of thought patterns tend to cause overthinkers to want to go to the garden to eat worms, or causes them to begin to believe the negativity they are thinking about themselves.

These thoughts tend to center around their believed inadequacies and inabilities in every and all situations, relationships, and scenarios. For instance, these types of thoughts tend to present themselves like, "I will never get better," "this situation will never improve," or "I am not capable." Now, none of these thoughts tend to be completely intentional, although self-sabotage can be associated with overthinking. However, in the early stages, most overthinkers actually use obsession as a way to try and problem solve and attempt to stop their worrying about things they cannot control (Relf, 2020).

What makes obsessive thoughts even more pervasive is that they have this awful ability to affix themselves to actual aspects of your life, making your personal awareness of where and how you overthink (if at all) that much harder to decipher. As seen in the above examples, obsessive thoughts caused by overthinking have no rhyme or reason to them; they simply latch onto whatever they are able to.

We will discuss how those manifest in different areas of your life, but first, let's finish up the preliminary discussions by talking about anxiety.

Anxiety

The Merriam-Webster dictionary defines 'anxiety' as an: " apprehensive uneasiness or nervousness usually over an impending or anticipated ill: a state of being anxious" (Merriam-Webster, 2019). Anxiety has become a bit of a buzz-word lately, and that is not to diminish anyone's personal journey with anxiety, or even to belittle the actual necessity for understanding and recognizing anxiety and its multiple forms and manifestations within different people and their lives.

Actually, that statement is meant to be one of joy. No longer can people say that you are simply "overthinking things," or that "it is not that bad," because anxiety is bad. It is bad for you, and what it does to your brain long term. The problem is that unless it is a shared anxiety, such as the global pandemic of 2020, anxiety is not really something which can be shared or understood. Yes, people can use their own experiences with anxiety to help you —the previous statement was not at all suggesting that people cannot help you with anxiety—but what is trying to be explained here is how singular each person's anxiety is.

This makes it all the more applicable and easy for an overthinking mind to attach to. Just like with obsession, anxiety has certain incredibly justifiable manifestations and scenarios, where it is almost more concerning that you are not feeling anxiety, rather than feeling it. For example, a situation like that could be if you were in the middle of a massive physical confrontation. There are very, very few people who could be in a massive mob and not feel some form of anxiety or adrenaline rush, and those types of people are most likely not overthinkers.

So, if there are times where anxiety is a bit more 'normal,' then what does it look like with overthinkers? Well, as with obsession, it is not that it pops up in unnecessary or even unjustifiable moments. It is that anxiety becomes a daily occurrence, and it is the thought and action pattern that your brain continues to thrive on; it has become the first, maybe even only response. Yes, this is also what suffering with anxiety can potentially look like, and sometimes overthinking does lead to problems with obsession, anxiety, and depression. Which is why obsession and anxiety are being more thoroughly discussed in this chapter.

Understanding that anxiety and obsession are strong emotional thoughts which are uniquely singular to you and how your brain functions with those emotions, plus the overthinking stimuli of your brain, is what makes you unique. It is also the main thing you need to begin analyzing and understanding about yourself. Having these thoughts more than 'normal' people is not a bad thing. Overthinking and being an anxious person does not make you less of a functioning adult. It simply means that your brain is not being kind to you, and you are going to have to put work into fixing that in order to have a better life in the long term.

Your brain is stuck. It is as simple as that. How you got to being stuck is irrelevant in this immediate moment (it will be important later). Right now, all you need to do is recognize that unfortunately, due to these anxious and obsessive thoughts, your overthinking brain has allowed itself to program these thoughts into literally everything, or that one particular part, of your life, and it is going to be hard to train it to let go.

How It Affects Your Life

This brings us to how overthinking, anxiety, and obsessive thoughts affect your life. Chances are, they have been affecting your life more than you know or are willing to admit to yourself. Now is not the time to continue in denial, even if it is just to yourself and the journal for this section, be honest. Really look at your life, your brain, your habits, your fears, and your triggers. Begin to look at the examples and see if anything manifests with you; no similarity is too small.

The whole point of this segment is to look and see where your overthinking has latched onto, and how it is causing you to behave.

The Habit

Habits may seem like an odd thing to mention, since we are discussing how overthinking manifests itself into your life, but that's just it. It is a habit. Remember the introduction? By obsessively thinking and allowing those thoughts to come in, your brain was building strong negative neural pathways which caused this type of thinking to become a habit. A very bad one.

Regardless of whether you intentionally built this habit or not (it would surprise many of you to know how often negative habits are built through unintentional actions), sadly, overthinking is a habit (Koa Foundations, n.d.). And it has manifested itself into your daily routine, however that looks.

The good news is that all habits can be changed, including negative mental ones. The bad news is that this will not be instantaneous, because it is going to require a lot of mental work to ensure that you make a good foundation on how to recognize your overthinking and what to do with it.

Relationships

Ah, relationships. The breeding ground of overthinking, anxieties, and obsessive thoughts for anyone, let alone someone who specifically deals with an overthinking brain. For this section, remember that what will be discussed here will be mainly for any type of relationship which is non-professional. This includes: family, friends, children, spouses, significant others, extended family, and even your peers and acquaintances (like the people at the gym or coffee shop).

So, the first question is, why is it so easy for overthinking, obsessive, and anxious thoughts to show up here? Because they involve other people. It sounds strange, but it is true. When you are combating an overthinking brain, an anxious brain, an obsessive brain, or a winning combination of all three, it is highly possible that another person is actually low-key stressing you out. This stress has absolutely nothing to do with the person, or even the relationship, necessarily. It more so has to do with the fact that unless your relationship is bordering on the over-communicative, there is a very good chance that sooner or later, you are going to begin questioning certain things in that relationship.

All it takes is that one wrong word, that one mis-step, or that one odd action in a daily occurrence to cause an overthinker's brain to begin going off like a firework display. Which, when you think about it, makes sense. By the very definition of an overthinker, they overthink something to the point where it becomes unhealthy (hence the obsession or anxiety). For example, let's say that you are an overthinker and the following happens:

Your friend Allen, whom you text faithfully every day (and normally throughout the day) about your troubles and anything and everything, does not text you back all morning. Not concerned, you send a text asking if they are okay and then go about your own work. However, there is still no reply at lunch. You are now beginning to feel anxious, and you start to wrack your brain to see if you can remember him mentioning anything about not being available for the day. Nothing comes to mind. By mid-afternoon, you are now an anxious mess, scrolling through your past text messages to see if there is some hidden clue in a well-placed emoji, comma, sentence, or word choice, to see if you had somehow annoyed them and had missed it. When that does not work, you begin to obsessively think and tear apart all of your previous conversations to see what went wrong. By the end of the day, you are convinced that they are no longer your friend and that the relationship is doomed, waiting for the strike of a masterful keystroke to end a friendship. You are devastated. However, by evening, Allen texts you back saying that he had forgotten his phone at home, and had to stay late at work in meetings and asks about your day. Completely forgetting the entire day you just spent filled with anxiety and negative thoughts, you answer Allen, and suddenly everything is alright with the world.

Does this type of scenario sound familiar to you? All it took was one change in a normal daily occurrence and then a lack of response to your inquiries to trigger a downward spiral of obsessive, anxious, and overthinking thoughts.

Now, before showing where things went wrong, let's go through some positives first. Take note of these positives, add them to your journal at the end of this segment, and meditate on how you can use these in a future chapter. The first positive is that you noticed your friend had not texted you and instead of immediately thinking you did something, you asked if they were okay.

It is hard with an overthinking, obsessive, and anxious brain, but sometimes when a regular relationship is different, it has absolutely nothing to do with you. They could be having a bad day or have a rushed morning. Asking and clarifying with them first is a great way to show you care and stave off overthinking tendencies.

The second positive is that you were able to not overthink the question. This step will take a while to get to, but once you get there, it is a really nice place to be. What is this step? It is simple. This step was how you asked Allen if he was okay, then went back to work. Some might find this a little stand-offish, and perhaps even rude, but going back to work and not allowing yourself to worry until lunch time (in the example) is a great exercise for an overthinker's brain, because it is allowing the other person to respond to your question without you beginning to create a narrative in your head, or come up with situations that would cause a negative mental cycle, which would cause your day to go downhill.

The third positive was how you went back through your text history and memory to see if Allen had mentioned not being available, and you had temporarily forgotten. Misremembering or forgetting that type of information is totally natural; we all do it sometimes, and then we are able to laugh it off when we remember and go about our day. Making this the third step before overthinking and worrying is another great way to begin gaining perspective and maintaining a slight bit of sanity before the overthinking takes hold.

Okay, so with those positives out of the way, it is time to start looking at the overthinking, obsession and anxiety thoughts, all of which were pretty obvious to see. Notice in the example how the longer Allen kept quiet, the worse the negative mental cycles became? You started to tear apart the texts looking for hidden clues, and then by the end of the day, you had convinced yourself that you had somehow upset Allen to the point where he would not even tell you what was wrong, and were already in the mourning period for that relationship.

Talk about a mental and emotional roller coaster. Now, again, this is not your fault in the sense that while you willingly chose to think that way, we are going to assume that you have had years (and maybe some actual experiences) to prove that this kind of thinking is accurate. Yes, you made the conscious choice to begin mourning the relationship with Allen, but not only did you stave off your overthinking for a short period of time, you most likely were even unaware of the mental thoughts which caused you to begin obsessing over every line of text and emojis.

But are you not tired of thinking this way? As someone who fights overthinking daily, it is exhausting just remembering the constant mental circles and emotional rides the brain can take you on if you are not in control of it. But do not be fooled, it takes a long time to get there, and the journey will involve looking into yourself and how that type of thinking got in.

Job

Overthinking is often something which pops up in the workforce, and that could be for a variety of valid reasons, such as a lack of communication between managers, staff, and business requirements, or perhaps it is because there was a conflict which was never fully resolved. Unfortunately, the corporate world has many, many reasons and ways where overthinking becomes an actual form of self-defense. However, since overthinkers tend to use the overthinking mental cycle to bring up negative thoughts and end up believing them, this can take a relatively toxic predisposition for a certain environment, and make it hundreds of times worse.

Compared to other manifestations of overthinking, it can become pretty obvious when you are overthinking in your job, because it will have a direct correlation to your performance. For instance, you can longer handle deadlines, you need to be overinformed on projects to the point where you are micromanaging other people, you cannot sleep, and you have problems making decisions, even when you used to make those decisions with barely any effort (Malin, 2021).

While to many people these symptoms could appear to be burnout (overthinking and burnout can be related and happen at the same time), there are finite differences. Essentially, burnout results in a lack of incentive, whereas overthinking causes you to freeze and be unable to finish. Both scenarios result in you fighting to complete a work-related project, but the reasonings behind completing the action are different. Consider the following examples:

James cannot handle deadlines at his job. He will know about a deadline months in advance, but continue to push off completing the project until the very last minute, because that is the only way he is able to think clearly and succinctly about what has to be done, and how.

For every project that he works on, Avery needs absolutely every possible piece of information, including the things that he does not need to know in order to complete his share of the work. If any task or project requires him to do input without having every possible scenario covered, Avery is unable to do the project without multiple team member's input and help.

Alison is normally a very good decision maker at work, and as a manager, she should be. However, something has changed. Every time a decision has to be made, Alison freezes and becomes unable to see the clear outcomes of each choice, and has developed a sense of 'buyers remorse' when she actually does make a decision at work. Even if it is the right decision, she will doubt that it was the right one for the project or her team.

Each person mentioned in the examples above exhibits how their overthinking has hindered something which is a requirement for their job, and in some cases, was something that they had not previously struggled with. James, for instance, cannot work on a project until it is right to the deadline, which has become a coping mechanism to combat the overthinking he experiences while working on the project. Avery is unable to get out of his head enough to be able to handle spontaneous projects, meaning his overthinking brain has developed perfectionism and analysis paralysis. Alison has developed overthinking to the point where she now doubts her decisions, which used to not occur.

When reading it on paper, it is pretty obvious in each instance where overthinking has hindered someone's ability to work, but it can be pretty hard to spot when the overthinking is within your own brain, or the overthinker is someone you know very well. The key with workplace overthinking is to gain perspective and hindsight on when to notice if you are overworked, overstressed, or overthinking, and that is something that comes with self-awareness and hindsight.

Physical and Extracurricular Activity

Many people understand and agree that overthinking takes over every part of their lives, yet physical activity or extracurricular activities is not often thought of when making that statement. Part of it is because it takes so much longer to begin noticing how overthinking hurts those parts of our lives.

For instance, with physical activity, overthinking may not come in until much later, because being active gives your brain a rush of endorphins, or 'happy hormones,' which allow your brain to stave off any type of negative spiral downwards. When overthinking does finally cross the threshold into our physical activities, it is so easily guised as a 'bad day,' a 'sign we need to take more rest days,' or 'leveling up.' Think about it. In any of those above scenarios, our brains are constantly fighting any type of negative thought combined with the ever-so optimistic 'if only' scenario to create the juxtaposition that we have to change something in order to be better. For many of us, we do make that change, and we do become better. But what about those times when we do not become better? What about when we let those defeatist thoughts win, or cause us to change how we approach the activity?

That right there, is how overthinking can hurt your physical activity. It is all well and good to think about your limits and begin to realistically contemplate if the next step of your physical journey is one you want to take, but when we let those thoughts become more negative than normal, the spiral begins.

Consider this example:

You have been doing this physical activity for a few years now, and you know that you have been improving, but then you hit a natural plateau. Unphased for a while, you push through, take more rest days, and begin to prepare for when your body is able to hurtle to the next level. but that leveling up is taking longer than you thought. Over the next few weeks, your thoughts are less optimistic and more pessimistic, you begin to start failing at things you had no problem completing before, and your previous "I can do it" thoughts become more negative and self-loathing, such as "Wow, now I cannot even do this, I am doing great" (infuse lots of anger and sarcasm into that statement).

Notice how in this example everything started out great. You were preparing for the level up, you were doing everything right, but when it took longer than you thought, that was when you let your guard down and allowed overthinking and a negative downward spiral to get to you. Do not worry; it is highly acknowledged that it is all fine and dandy to sit here typing that statement out, but you are the one actually feeling it. Well, believe it or not, that feeling has been felt in physical activities before. Many times. Combating and fighting the overthinking aspect, while also dealing with physical inadequacies or extra training to meet certain goals, is not fun. Which is where accountability partners or safe people come into play. Doing physical activity with upbeat people will help combat your overthinking and help you begin to implement practices which will be discussed in a future chapter.

And with that, onto the extracurricular activities, or, for the context of this book, social activities. When it comes to social circles, clubs, or activities where being social is the main objective, it is pretty easy for overthinking to sneak in there. The problem is that compared to a relationship, overthinking presents itself differently in how we handle it. For most people, overthinking in regards to a club or some type of social extracurricular activity results in no longer participating, or being delayed or avoidant of that situation. This happens because the negative downward spiral has caused you to begin believing all of the awful things your brain has been telling you.

For instance: Laura has been part of her boating club for years. She enjoys the activity and the people, and normally has a great time. She is even on the committee and helps out with fundraisers and maintaining the boats in the off season. However, due to circumstances which were out of her control, some of the last few fundraisers did not bring in as much money as they would normally, and Laura had begun to feel self-conscious about it. This caused her overthinking to begin working its way into how she thought about the club and her role in it. Over the next few weeks, members and friends noticed that Laura was not as chipper, and had begun to not be at the club as often. She had also begun to skip meetings and was not as attentive or involved in planning events like before.

Again, notice how all it took was one negative thing and Laura's brain was able to easily push overthinking into that area of her life. In this instance, Laura's overthinking caused her to withdraw, most likely due to thoughts of her not being good enough and feeling like someone else would do a better job at those events than her. The more her thoughts spiraled, the more she withdrew.

In each example, overthinking was not immediately present; and this is something that you really need to notice and pay attention to. Just because you are an overthinker does not necessarily mean it will take over every area of your life immediately. It definitely has the ability to, and for some people it sadly will, but for the lucky few, there may be a few areas of their lives that are insulated from that type of thinking.

Normally, that is because those areas of life have little room for negativity, either because there are too many happy emotions and thought processes related to it already, or the opportunity has not arisen.

This is important: You cannot be lazy in watching how you think in those areas. As you saw in the examples—and as you have learned—overthinking can creep into anything if you give it space to. Including areas of your life which are currently just fine.

Thankfully, once you have become comfortable fighting your overthinking, it will become a habit, and you will not have to pay special attention to these areas of your life.

Journal

Well, this chapter was a lot to take in. Now we come to the good stuff. It is time for you to make a cup of tea or coffee and begin to really think about everything you have read in this chapter.

Did you notice any similarities in the examples? If so, what were they? Let your thoughts and mind wander down that trail for a bit. You could be surprised by what comes up.

Next up, remember those positive attributes that were in some examples? Pull them up and begin to look at them again. Notice how these positive actions are small and easy to add as a step to stop your overthinking brain from immediately jumping into crisis mode. Write down the ones that really resonate with you, and begin to come up with mantras, or ways to remind yourself to use them before overthinking.

Finally, look at the areas of your life (if any) where you do not overthink.

Make a special point of keeping these areas of your life in the front of your brain in the coming chapters.

Chapter 3

Eliminate Through Awareness

It may seem a bit like an oxymoron, since part of overthinking is that you are hyper-aware of your brain and yourself, but there is a common trend which has been peeking up and throughout all of the previous parts of this book so far. Your hyper-aware, overthinking brain is only aware of the negatives around you. From the negatives about the situation, to hyper-focusing on all of the negatives about you personally, there have probably been very few moments where your brain has allowed you to be positive and actually find a usable solution.

It is in those moments where awareness comes in. Being aware is so much more than noticing when you are on a negative cycle, or that you are beginning to overthink; even though that is a good place to start. However, to truly begin combatting your overthinking brain, you need to be aware of everything around it. You need to be aware of what you are overthinking about, why you are overthinking about it, and how your brain has decided to overthink to 'solve' the problem or circumstance that is facing.

It takes time to get to this stage. It could take you weeks, months, maybe even years. But the hard work and consistency that you put into figuring out and building up your awareness consistently—even through your overthinking phases—will pay off. Just like with so many other things in our lives, what you put into this section of your overthinking journey, will directly correlate into what comes out of it.

Why You Need It

Some of you may be wondering why you even need self-awareness. Being self-aware of your overthinking may seem like enough, but in reality, it is not. Many overthinkers are aware that they overthink; they may even be aware of when they are actually overthinking. The problem is that when your brain is overthinking, it has the ability to turn into a runaway train. Everyone knows what is happening, but no one is able to stop it. Your brain has become that powerful because you consciously, or unconsciously, continue to dwell on those negative thoughts and related thought patterns. However, do not worry. Your brain is able to bounce back; it will just require more effort and awareness on your part to tear down those habits and put new ones in place. The good news is that once you have created new mental pathways and habits, it will become easier to stick to those than to return to overthinking over time.

Awareness and Overthinking

Normally, awareness is used as an overall term to describe your ability to understand and know yourself. Being aware is how our brains naturally begin to grow, change, and adapt to circumstances that are new, or need us to change in order to do something. That is, in fact, exactly how awareness will be used in this book; just on a deeper level. To truly combat overthinking with awareness, you need to be able to understand when and why you are overthinking. You need to be able to understand and differentiate between when you are going into negativity, worrying, fixating, ruminating, obsessing, or your anxiety cycles while you are overthinking. You need to understand what triggered it, and most of all, you will need the awareness and ability to go back to that scenario or situation later on and gain hindsight on what triggered the overthinking.

Understanding how you personally begin to overthink brings up a new step of self-awareness, because it will help you catch yourself as your overthinking begins to take over. Similarly, you need to begin implementing habits to stop your overthinking, or to go back to those episodes where you can apply hindsight. Figuring out why certain things triggered you will be crucial in your ability to stop overthinking and to begin rewiring your brain to not overthink in the face of those triggers.

Gaining that next level of awareness in regards to your overthinking is going to be a journey. It will not be easy to see how fragile certain parts of your emotions or mind are, or have gotten over time, but embracing that vulnerability through awareness and deciding to strengthen it through change and habit in fighting overthinking will help you turn the corner mentally.

Implementing Awareness

When it comes to implementing awareness, you have to understand that it will start as a chore which will eventually become a habit. Just like how overthinking is a habit, everything you are going to do to combat it, will also overtime become a habit. The replacement habit, if you will.

The other problem with implementing awareness is that in order to use it to stop your overthinking, you have to actually start becoming present in your everyday life. The good news is that this is now something everyone deals with, thanks to the rise of technology, social media, the news, and constant distractions from our smart devices and how often they are in our hands, or on our person. With so many distractions, it is pretty easy to not stay present in every single moment of the day, which is actually quite sad, when you think about it. Or, so many of us are so busy with our lives that we are constantly thinking one to three steps ahead. Our days become a list, and we tell ourselves we will enjoy life when we are done, but we are never done. No matter which of these scenarios it is, overthinking brains have it hundreds of times worse, because they are either so busy fixating on something else or shutting down from being overwhelmed that being in the present is like looking directly into a stage spotlight. It is blinding, it is painful, and it (the brain) does not want to do it.

Understandable. The present is most likely where overthinking is being triggered and therefore something painful, unresolved, or activating has happened; and although being present in that scenario is never fun, you have to start doing it. Your awareness will not develop and persist in tougher situations if you do not begin to build that habit now.

Finding the time and ways to be present is tricky, but definitely worth the effort. Introducing ways to be present really depends on where you notice that you disassociate the most, but here are a few quick tips to get you started. First, you can begin to practice being more present by taking several deep and intentional breaths. Pay attention to your body and your surroundings as you breathe, and come back to the present rather than hiding in your brain. Second, you can pay more attention to your surroundings by stopping any type of multitasking. Part of the reason we are not always present is because our brains are already so busy making sure we finish everything we said we would do, while not dying (like texting and crossing the street), that being present is absolutely not an option. Third, you can accept things as they are. That is it. Just accept. Do not try to change, do not try to adapt, do not even necessarily react. Just be there and accept it.

Before going any further, we need to iron something out. This chapter and section is the build up for the next chapter (as it is with all books); however, here we are going to specifically discuss how to implement the habit of awareness in your life. This habit of awareness is going to then be subsumed into the next chapter, meaning that the next chapter is written with the understanding that you have begun the steps listed below, to start building and implementing your self-awareness.

How to Build a Habit

So, before discussing ways to begin implementing awareness into your mental patterns, we are going to briefly discuss how to even successfully implement a habit. Some of you may be incredibly familiar with this concept, and if that is so, feel free to skip this section. But just in case this is something many of you have not consciously done in a while, here are a few things to know and do to be successful.

First is understanding how long it takes. It takes roughly 21 days to make a habit, and about 90 days to make it into a pattern or unconscious decision. If you have done anything in the world of physical fitness, this pattern and concept will not be new to you. However, with those specific 'deadlines' in place, open up a calendar and begin mapping out how long some of these things might take for you if you started today, next week, or even next month. Visually seeing how long it will take you might seem a bit disheartening, but do not let that get to you. Everyone has the same timeline, and no one is exempt from that length of time in creating or maintaining a new habit and fostering it into a lifestyle. You are not alone, and you can do this. But you need to be aware of the long-haul you are in for.

Alright, now onto the nitty gritty stuff.

Start Small

Picking a small thing to do consistently that will not add to your stress, or become an hour-long new blocked out time in your calendar, is one of the ways you can ensure that your habits actually stick. When it comes to awareness, this could be something like implementing a five-minute daily check-in with yourself on your commute home, after dinner, or before bed. If you decide to use this example, make sure that you set a timer. This will ensure you are not creating a scheduled overthink time of your day, while allowing your overthinking brain time to adjust itself and bringing in self-awareness in your day. It is amazing what even allowing five minutes of non-fixation thinking can do for your brain to help it feel refreshed and actually more willing to be mindful throughout the upcoming days.

Small Note

Now, if there are moments, days, or times when these five minutes become negative, that is okay. Sometimes we need to be negative to get the negativity out. But be sure to use your practice at awareness to acknowledge your feelings without letting them spiral out of control.

Practice Daily

If you ever practiced an instrument, or trained for specific fitness goals, you know there are unlimited benefits to practicing something daily, even if it is for brief periods of time. Low-key, daily practice (especially when you are just starting out) will help your body and mind tolerance and discipline grow with you. Using the example of the five-minute awareness check-in, if you practice it daily, you may be able to up that time to 10 minutes after a few weeks, and so on and so forth. When it comes to awareness, daily practice will also help clear your brain and give you the ability to begin upping the awareness to become a constant, subconscious frame of mind (which is what we want), to help you combat overthinking before it even starts.

Stack Your Habits

This may sound a bit odd, but stacking a habit is putting a new habit onto an old habit or routine, to help ensure it actually sticks with you for longer than the original 21 days. Thankfully, there are many apps which can help you build this kind of routine and begin to stack habits on top of each other. Continuing with the example of practicing five-minute awareness check-ins daily, you could stack that habit onto any pre-existing habit like your commute to and from work, your post-work workout, or your nighttime routine to wind down from your day.

No matter how you go about introducing awareness into your life, remember, it is a habit. Specifically, it is going to be the habit to replace overthinking (along with a few others which will be mentioned later). Remember: Nature hates a vacuum, so if you do not have something to replace your overthinking with, you are going to end up right back where you started.

Stop!

Which brings us to the first way to implement awareness. Quite simply: stop. Stop overthinking.

This does not mean stop overthinking in general, because that would be pretty hard (and uncomfortable) to do immediately if you do not have a backup way of thinking. What is meant is to take the reins of when you are overthinking and consciously stop your brain when it begins to go down a negative spiral. This is where your newfound awareness habit comes into play. Being aware of when you are overthinking will allow you to stop. You may not stop immediately, and you may not stop for the entire day, but beginning to notice your thoughts and stop them will go a long way in future steps.

Also, remember: You may slip a few times and you may not catch your overthinking every single time in the beginning. That is okay. This practice is something which will grow with you the longer you do it. So do not give up, and keep going.

Slow Down

Immediately after stopping your thoughts, slow them down. Part of the reason our brains are able to get away with overthinking is because it is a whirlwind. One minute we are simply worrying about an incredibly valid thing, and then next thing we know, we are suddenly on this runaway brain train on thoughts and negative cycles we were not even aware were a problem (sometimes).

Forcing your brain to slow down will allow you to notice where your overthinking brain is going, and to continue consciously stopping those thoughts. this step is incredibly hard and takes a lot of focus, energy, and practice. How to slow down your thoughts is easier said than done. It is to simply begin to almost snail-like process each individual thought and emotion that is going through your brain. Implementing it really depends on what works for you. Some people prefer to get into an almost meditative state through closed eyes and deep breathing, some prefer to go to a quiet space, or to put in earphones. For other people, it is achieved through sheer determination and willpower. Finding the method that works for you will be a trial and error type of method, but once you find it, you have struck gold.

Take Control of Your Emotions

Slowing down your thoughts will then allow you to implement the next step of self-awareness: controlling your emotions. Our emotions are hard to control because so many of them are instantaneous reactions to something happening around us. They sometimes happen without us even fully recognizing that that is what we have done.

A great way to stop this type of emotional reaction is to stop and slow down your brain. Slowing your brain and its thoughts will allow you the space to begin evaluating what emotion you are using and reacting with, and even give you the ability to recognize and decide if that is the right or appropriate emotion for the scenario.

Honestly, this will not happen all of the time. Even people with gold-level awareness will still cry or scream when frightened or in an incredibly high-risk situation. Being calm in those moments takes years of training, and is something that you not only have to work up to, but something you would repeatedly have to put yourself into to create and maintain. Which is not what this book is discussing. In this step, we are discussing the ability to not immediately lash out, either verbally or in our minds, when someone slights us, or to be able to notice and dissect our emotions when we notice we are overthinking and continuing a worry or maintain a negative cycle in our minds.

Before some of you begin to think that controlling your emotions means to stop them, that is absolutely not what is being said here. Controlling your emotions is simply being able to decide what emotion you are going to think with and which one you are going to act on. Being hurt or upset when there is an actual slight or wrong against you is completely valid and something you should never be ashamed of. It is how you react to it and display those emotions where things can get a bit messy. Whether you know it or not, overthinking in response to a trigger is actually a display of those emotions, even if you are the only one to witness the overthinking. At the end of the day, overthinking is a reaction to someone's action or a situation; and you can have complete control over those. Being upset is valid. Being angry is valid. Overthinking those scenarios to the point where your anxiety, depression, or any other type of negative thinking—while valid because you are still feeling them—is maybe not the healthiest way for you to process those emotions.

Journal

Now that you are armed with ways to build your self-awareness, it is time to begin deep diving into yourself. Ask yourself these questions and think about them for a while. Let your brain and emotions begin to really look into the answers.

- How self-aware are you right now?

- How can you implement self-awareness daily?

- Is there a pre-existing habit you can stack it onto?

- How are you going to remind yourself to stop when you notice that you are starting to overthink?

- How are you going to begin slowing down your thoughts to control your emotions?

- Are you willing to begin learning to try and control your emotions?

- Do you need or have an accountability partner?

CHAPTER 4

The Quickest Way to Stop Overthinking

Stopping something like overthinking has essentially two parts to it. The first, which is covered in this chapter, discusses actual tactics and things you can begin doing immediately, or within the relative short-term, to begin the journey. The second step, which is covered in the next chapter, deals with more long-term continuations of what is discussed in the first step.

This chapter is going to build on what was discussed in the previous one in regards to self-awareness. Meaning, that these steps are going to assume that you are working on building and strengthening your mental awareness, and will have steps to which will include that type of mindset and practice. Additionally, how you go about building and implementing your self-awareness (i.e. the section on how to implement and build habits) will be incredibly useful for beginning to start the following principles and changes in your current mind patterns.

Cognitive Replacement

Have you ever heard of the saying that nature abhors a vacuum? What it is referring to is the concept that everything in this world, from nature to our inner bodies, has an action and reaction balance, and when that balance is put off-kilter, something adapts to replace what originally goes missing. You can see this in the world with how animals adapt to being around cities (i.e. birds needing new nesting spots, so finding them on condominium balconies or in trees they normally would not use), to how our bodies adapt to not having certain enzymes or abilities. The same is said for your mind. Fixing overthinking is not simply to just stop and go about your day. Your brain will not handle that well because there is now all of this unused energy, thought patterns, and intention on what your brain was about to do.

Which is where cognitive replacement comes in. Cognitive replacement is essentially replacing a way your brain thinks or behaves. This could be something as simple as rewiring your brain for how it attempts problem solving, to trying to create more intentional focus times by stopping or rerouting daydreams to pre-allocated time periods. In regards to overthinking, cognitive replacement is replacing your overthinking thoughts with something different.

Preferably these replacement thoughts are positive and more helpful to your brain, day, and overall processes than what your overthinking has so far brought to the table. Yes, that sounds harsh, and it was meant to. Your overthinking brain, while there are times it is incredibly justifiable, has not done you any favors in regards to your mental health and how you are able to think. Yes, you can do this. No, becoming an overthinker was not your goal, intention, or really your fault. But at the same time, you have continued it—consciously or unconsciously—and it is time to grab a hold of it and begin to change that pattern. Starting with cognitive replacement.

Building off of the habits section in the last chapter, begin to think of ways that you can proactively begin to put cognitive replacement into your daily routine. This could be like implementing a gratitude practice when your brain begins to start a negative trajectory, or having a scrap of paper beside you to write out what you are frustrated with and how you can actually begin to solve that problem. Cognitive replacement does not have to be this grand, 12-step program. It can be as difficult or as easy as you want it to be.

Since we are starting off easy and with the little things; it is really recommended that you choose the easy route.

Self-Awareness and Hindsight

As mentioned in the previous chapter, self-awareness is one of the key ingredients in fighting overthinking and stopping those brain patterns. Including hindsight into your self-awareness tactics will be a great way to step up your awareness progress as well as to begin to retrain your mind to find new forms of awareness to begin implementing.

In case this is a term that is new to you, hindsight refers to looking back at a scenario, conversation, or even an emotion, to figure out the cause, why and how you felt and reacted that way, and if that reaction was what you wanted to exhibit; and if not, how you can change that for next time.

Hindsight is a great learning tool to help overcome overthinking because it forces you to break down scenarios into piece-by-piece mini-bites of compacted information. You take one action and bundle it with your thoughts and feelings about that action, then begin to analyze how and why it worked or not. This also provides you with a great self-learning technique which can be used in future instances.

For example: Josh was having a frustrating day at work. Everything that could go wrong was going wrong. During his lunch break, Josh took a moment to look back at some of the scenarios he had just gone through, to see how he had handled them. While analyzing, he noted that most of the interactions and reactions were handled well on his end, and only one was a bit negative and had caused him to begin spiraling slightly. Even though he had caught the beginnings of his overthinking spiral, Josh took a look at that incident more closely.

It was about a special work project with a few of his team members. The project was not going well and one of the team members was blatantly ignoring Josh's role in the group, which was to edit the other person's work. This had been going on for awhile, but today, on top of everything else, the person's attempts at justifying their inability to do what Josh needed them to do were just too much. While he did not yell at them, Josh was definitely short and a little more curt than he normally was. After the team member had left, Josh had then unintentionally spent 10 minutes mentally fuming at his co-worker and getting nothing done. In the present, Josh was analyzing why he had been so short-tempered with his coworker and that entire interaction. He mentally acknowledged his frustrations and made a note in his day timer to talk with their manager about how team roles could be changed, or needed to be enforced, and then began to look at his emotions and reactions. Josh studied what had made him so frustrated, what he was responsible for in that frustration, and what he could do to begin minimizing those frustrations and his actions in the future. Additionally, he began to identify certain triggers, and walked through scenarios on how he could avoid being that short-tempered in the future (if at all possible). He also went and apologized to his co-worker after lunch.

This was a bit of a long example, so let's break it down. We will start off with the positives first. In this example, Josh immediately recognized that he needed to re-analyze and evaluate the scenario with his coworker. This is a good thing, because it shows Josh's self-awareness and his recognition that hindsight (or being more removed from that scenario) would help him be able to figure out responsibilities and give a fresh outlook on things. Josh also recognized and validated his frustrations. Nowhere in this book can it be said that your emotions are invalid. However, Josh recognized that while his emotions were valid, his reaction and response to them, were not. Additionally, Josh took his frustrations and made a proactive action out of them by making a note to discuss this coworker with a manager, to try and resolve the issue. Next, Josh then began to parse over the interaction to decide what was his responsibility (also known as boundary), and which of those responsibilities he could fix or help with, compared to what he was not responsible for. Josh then began to make plans for how to avoid and fix his boundaries or frustrations in the future, and then ended that entire thought session by apologizing to his coworker.

Small Note

Some of you may think that the apology to the coworker was unnecessary, and that is a case-by-case and personal decision. In this instance, it was necessary, because the coworker received more frustration from Josh than was appropriate for the situation.

As you can see through this example, hindsight is an excellent tool to combat overthinking. An overthinking brain with no control or good habits would have taken that scenario and made it worse (most likely in their own minds) by fixating on all of the negatives of the situation and how it is making everything else worse, etc. While Josh never denied that possibility, he also did not fixate on that possibility. Rather, he used hindsight to begin owning up to his own mistakes, where things could have gone better on his end, and made plans on how he could better himself in the future.

Focus on What Can Go Right

This may sound a little too much like, "Focus on the bright side!" in terms of how to think, and while there are definitely elements of that mentality in this section, it does not go that far. Part of the problem with overthinkers is that they normally only focus on the negatives of life (it is pretty rare to find an overthinker who is positive, normally those are just incredibly hopeful optimists). Compared to overthinkers, who are predominantly negative, and hopeful optimists, who border on too positive, there is a happy middle ground. Which is: focusing on what can go right.

Thankfully, this sounds exactly like what you are meant to do. Combatting overthinking is essentially everything you can possibly do to ensure that the negativity your brain is so used to producing is only produced when required. Including making the concentrated effort on noting when things can actually go right, or what you can do to make things go right. This can be something as simple as reminding yourself that it does not have to be that bad, that it may not actually be that bad, or that there is goodness in the world.

A great example would be to come up with one singular thing that you know is right and positive to begin combatting overthinking. For instance, say that your brain tends to overthink in the form of self-loathing, and the thought, "I suck at social interactions" is a common thought you have when things go wrong. You can focus on what can go right by battling that thought with, "I might be a bit awkward, but sometimes things go okay and I have a good time."

When it comes to focusing on what can go right, you really need to start small. It is very, very easy to turn your overthinking brain into a brain that has latched onto toxic positivity, which then continues the cycle in a different way. Practice doing what the above example mentions, which is turning a negative overthinking pattern into an acknowledgement of the foundational truth, tacked on with a positive from past experiences. This will begin to help your brain notice when the overgeneralizations of your negative thought patterns have begun, validate your feelings of the overgeneralizations, and then begin to combat the negative overgeneralizations with known, true, positives.

The Right Perspective

Perspective is always key. It helps us understand other people, get to the bottom of our own feelings, and even help us begin to expect how some people will react or behave in certain situations. It is also key with overthinking, as it will start to force an overthinking brain to acknowledge where the overthinking has started and where that train of thought is wrong.

When we are on a negative spiral from overthinking, our brain is completely unaware; and frankly, no longer cares about the perspective for that scenario, comment, action, or thought, and how anything came about. It is simply following the mental path it has been building for a long time. Adding perspective can act like that big red "STOP" sign we see on the road. It causes overthinking to actually begin to stop, because the feelings and thoughts it is causing us to have are suddenly put into question.

Again, not in the way that those emotions are not valid, but rather into the question of whether those emotions are actually based off of the original triggering scenario. You have most likely noticed this yourself. When our brains are in overthinking mode, they are no longer fully aware of how things connect, because the negative spiral is a pre-existing mental pathway our brains have found loads of ways onto, and they do not really care how they get there. When you suddenly put perspective into the triggering event, you are able to give your brain a jolt out of its predetermined state and actually begin considering what it is thinking and why. It is pretty hard to continue beating yourself up mentally when perspective reminds your brain that you were originally upset about something completely unrelated.

Sometimes that jolt of reality is exactly what we need to implement the other good habits which have been discussed so far in this book, and it will certainly go a long way in helping you instill the other good habits that will be discussed in the upcoming chapters.

Now, here is the kicker—the perspective that you use has to be the right perspective; that does not mean right-wing, or the right answer. It has to be right as in, that was the reality of what has happened. This type of perspective is sometimes hard to remember or input because it is forcing our brain to remember a very recent traumatic or triggering event. However, there are many times where our overthinking brains need to be hit upside the head with a reality check (also known as perspective). Even if that reality is not pleasant, or is something we do not want to return to. Going back to the 'scene of the crime' as it were, in our minds, can provide numerous benefits. It can reinforce the facts (which our overthinking brains have probably ignored or skewed), it can remind us of why we were originally upset (or think of it as a reset to try and find an actual solution), and it can get us out of our negative mental downhill spiral.

Implementing this tactic to stop overthinking will be one of the harder things to do, because it will require a lot of mental honesty and transparency. Please note how that was not a green light to continue mentally beating yourself up. Even people who have long since gotten their overthinking under control still have a hard time implementing the right perspective in their minds. Why? Because this perspective is going to be so transparent with where we went wrong, what we did wrong, where we could have been better, or where we began to overthink. It is going to cause you to see, in real-time, your failures and vulnerabilities. Which is exactly where your overthinking comes in. Funny how one of the things we use to stop overthinking can actually be because of it as well. Just remember to do your best, and try to be self-aware of your thoughts and what caused them.

Being Aware of Your Emotions

This step is intricately tied to many parts of this book, but it was put in this chapter because being in tune with your emotions—including when you are overthinking—is a quick way to stop actually overthinking. Being aware of your emotions is also different from self-awareness, because this particular step requires that you are aware of what emotions caused you to spiral, and to accept them.

There you have it.

One of the biggest ways to combat your overthinking is not just to give new and positive thoughts to your brain, but also to accept the emotions which caused you to spiral out of control in the first place. Misplaced or ignored emotions bottle up inside of us, and how they come out is messy, harmful, and normally in a scenario which we openly admit did not deserve that type of outburst. While you may think that overthinking does not do that, as we now know, that is not always the case. Being aware of, and accepting every emotion you have will begin to stop that subconscious emotional bottle-and-explosion cycle that you most likely have on repeat.

Yes, it is very well acknowledged that this sounds way easier than it actually is. It is a lot of work to acknowledge and accept your emotions, because it requires that you actually think about why you are upset, and that is a path many of us do not want to go down. In all honesty, some of you may need professional help with this particular step, because it is so easy to believe that we have acknowledged and accepted our emotions when we really have not. It is only through the eyes of a professional or accountability partner who is really in tune with their own emotions who can tell the difference. Being aware of your emotions will go a long way in helping you combat overthinking, because you are going to start to get at the actual stem of why you overthink. It will force you to begin accepting and working on that past trauma, that past event or that reason, as to why overthinking is the solution your brain has come up with.

Journaling

So, the first question after reading this last section is, how many of you suddenly feel less of a desire to work on your overthinking minds, knowing all the work and specific emotional awareness it will require? Be honest.

There is no shame in seeing how much, and how hard, the work will actually be to combat overthinking and have moments of doubt, or an unwillingness to continue. Change is never easy, and it is guaranteed that those who have successfully gotten through it did doubt, stop, or want to stop, at one point in time. That is not a green light for you to actually stop, but acknowledging and helping you understand that you are not alone in wanting to (if you do) is not a bad thing either. We are all human, and sometimes the complicated emotions that go with that statement are just too much for us all the time.

So, take a break. Set a timer for five minutes and just let your mind wander. Make a cup of tea or coffee if you need to. But be sure to continue this book and to do the following journal prompts. Understanding yourself and implementing self awareness is hard. You are doing a fantastic job, and you can do this.

Out of all of the sections that have been discussed, which is the one that you are most keen to start right away? Pick that one, and then begin to write out one, small, daily actionable thing you can do from that segment in your daily routine to help begin building self-awareness.

How self-aware are you already? Where do you need to improve?

Were there parts of you that believe you may need more professional help with this section to combat your overthinking tendencies?

Chapter 5

Dump All Negative Thinking

Now that you have an understanding and the rudimentary conditioning on how to begin to stop overthinking, it is time to go onto the second step, which is to continue what was discussed in the previous chapter with a very specific goal: to dump all negative thinking and negative cycles.

It sounds almost too easy to be true (as has come to be one of the hallmarks of stopping overthinking), but halting your various types of negative spirals can do wonders for continuing to battle overthinking in the long run. As an overthinker, your brain is sadly already wired to be negative, which we saw when discussing the different manifestations of an overthinking brain. Obsessing, ruminating, worrying, and the cause of anxiety all combine towards negative mental habits. But then, what does this mean for your brain? Chances are you are already quite aware that this means your brain will begin to cycle down negative paths pretty quickly. Even the smallest slight or upset to your day, life, or scenario could trigger a negative mental spiral. Which is honestly most likely not something you are fully able to control, even if you are conscious of it. Your brain has become so accustomed to looking, implementing, and telling itself negative lies about itself, yourself, or life that it has become a really, really bad habit. One that you most likely cannot stop, even if you wanted to.

Yet, getting rid of, changing, altering, or replacing your mental negativity cycle is going to be one of your best paths to success; but it will also be the hardest. There is no sugar-coating this particular step, phase, or chapter. Battling and dumping your negativity cycle is going to most likely be one of the hardest things this book will prescribe for you. Let's face it; implementing everything which was discussed in the previous chapter is relatively easy to do right now because you are eager to start this journey. This book has ramped you up, and you are all set and ready to go. But what about when the momentum slows down, or you have an especially hard day? Or, what about when your brain will automatically begin a negativity cycle?

That is where due diligence, determination, and personal desire come in. All of which can be supplemented by beginning the habit of dumping all negative thinking.

The Negativity Cycle

The good news is that you are most likely aware of some of those spirals now, and may or may not have begun to analyze what triggered them and how your negativity particularly manifests itself. The fact that you are aware when you negatively spiral out of control and into deep bouts of depression, worrying, or whatever way your brain manifests overthinking, is a good thing (even though it really may not seem like it). Being aware is a good step, because this will allow you to begin taking hold of your thoughts and fighting them.

What is even better (in a manner of speaking) is that the negativity cycle is actually a very simple process of two steps. First, there is a triggering event, and second, your brain latches onto it and automatically begins to negatively spiral. The simplicity of the negativity cycle is a good thing, because there are actually less things for you to be aware of and combat. Even though they are incredibly hard, pervasive, and sneaky things, you only have two steps to be aware of and change.

So, then, what is the problem?

The problem is how easily your brain is now able to go into a negative spiral. Sure, there are definitely events, triggers, or scenarios where a negative spiral is actually really understandable and relatable. These things could be big life events like a massive breakup, a death, losing a job, or even moving to a new city and having to start all over. When our brains and bodies are overwhelmed, there is definitely a very, very strong urge to either be optimistic or negative. Not many people choose to be in the middle. Those scenarios—not that it is healthy to spiral out negatively—are almost easier to walk back out of, because the solutions to those spirals tend to be forced onto you; such as needing to find a new job, getting into a new relationship, healing yourself, or making friends and a new life in a new city.

But these types of events are most likely not what easily trigger you or someone you know into an overthinking negative mental spiral. Chances are, those triggers are actually tiny, little things, which to some people may be an innocent problem or a slight millisecond of frustration. Yet to an overthinking and negative brain, these events could be catastrophic. They could even be triggered by an innocent little negative thought like, "Oh, well isn't this just peachy?" (said with every inner frustration and sarcasm imaginable). It is really sad, and kind of scary, that this could actually be all it takes to convince your brain to begin a spiral into negativity: but there you have it. It is that easy. All it takes is that one particular moment, and everything positive which has actually happened to you that day becomes forgotten. Not that your brain would not acknowledge the positives of the day if it was reminded, but an overthinking brain on a negative spiral tends to forget those things exist until they are literally pushed to the forefront of the mind in an aggressive reminder.

Let's be honest, we have all been there, we have all had moments where those tiny little irritants are the one thing that wrecks our entire hour or maybe even day. The problem is that for an overthinking brain even this tiny little admission could potentially act like kryptonite for kick-starting your negativity cycle.

Why?

Coming full circle, the answer is because your brain is so accustomed to being negative. No, this does not mean you cannot validate any negativity you might be feeling, or that you need to create this fake and toxic form of positivity to stop the negative cycle. In order to actually dump and begin to combat your negativity cycle, you are going to have to exert a lot of self-control, self-awareness, and determination to get you through those tough moments.

Begin the Dump

This is where beginning to understand how to dump your negativity comes in. Essentially, what dumping your negativity looks like is a continuation of the cognitive replacement and heightening self-awareness suggestions from the previous chapter. According to the Calm Clinic, the steps to begin dumping all negative thoughts are as follows: installing and working on your awareness through identification and recording, finding the truth and analyzing your thoughts and feelings, disputing the negative thoughts, finding a positive replacement, and setting realistic goals (Abraham, 2022).

Small Note

Beginning to introduce cognitive replacement is tricky, and is not easily done alone. Be sure to keep someone in the loop during this stage, because the following steps could easily be overdone, become a replacement for negativity, introduce toxic positivity, or even become a new step in your brain's negativity cycle. That is not to say that you cannot do this alone, but if you are an extreme overthinker, even having a safe person who is aware of what you are attempting to help keep your mind clear and on the right track is highly recommended.

Identification and Recording

Awareness is the first step in beginning to dump your negative emotions. Creating the mental discipline and self-knowledge to be aware of your thoughts and feelings as they happen (for most of them, at least), will help you begin to identify when you are being negative and to spiral downwards.

The bad news is, just because you are aware does not necessarily mean that it will be any easier to stop your negative cycles. In fact, there may be a period of time where this is actually worse, because your brain is aware of what it is doing and what is happening, but your will and mind are still at war on what to do. You may be fighting the old habits of negativity with everything that has come up in this book so far, but your mind may not be completely accepting of these concepts.

For instance: Perhaps you have started to believe that you are actually really bad at a hobby you have been enjoying for the past few years.

Even though you are technically aware of getting better, your negativity cycle has caused you to not believe the cold, hard truth through videos, photos, or even statements from your peers. Being aware when your brain is in a negativity cycle, which is causing you to believe the negative lies about yourself that your brain is feeding you, is a good start. Now you have to go a step deeper.

Being mentally aware of what is happening is not enough. It is great for the moment, or to jolt you out of the beginnings of a spiral momentarily, but you have to do more. Start with recording the entire moment. Whether it be in the journal used for this book, an app, or even a voice memo, you need to write down the scenario, your feelings, and your thoughts, to be able to gain perspective on the big picture rather than letting your brain continue to trick you with negativity.

What this does is begin to separate your feelings and thoughts from the actual problem, which is where a lot of people are able to begin problem solving. Which is what will be discussed in the following steps (Abraham, 2022).

Analyze

After writing down what caused your negativity, how it began to manifest, and the scenario behind it, it is time for you to actually re-read what you have written and begin to look for patterns in these events. Do you see any similarities in anything? Like in the event, what was said, how you responded, how you reacted, or how you became negative about yourself?

These similarities will point toward your own unique mental pattern, and finding this pattern will help increase your self-awareness with the goal of beginning to stop your negativity spirals more quickly, and to plant the seeds for finding solutions to these moments.

Find the Truth

Building off of your self analysis, you are finally ready to begin actually combatting the lies you are telling yourself. Remember: Just because your brain has gotten really good at lying to you, does not mean that what it is telling you during a negativity cycle is true. Which sounds really scary while reading it on paper. How weird, awful, and just icky to feel and know that your brain can lie to you; but it happens quite often, sadly. Think about that friend who dated yet another loser, even though you knew it was a bad idea, but they insisted that this person was a good change. Or when a friend or family member started to believe those specific pills were working. Our brains are so smart, yet can be so easily deceived. Which is why we have to begin building pillars of truth and understanding to combat everything our brain latches onto and somehow begins to believe is real. Including when your brain is having a grand old time lying to you in a negativity cycle.

Remember those negative, ruminating, obsessive, anxious, and worrying thought examples from earlier? Thoughts like: how much you sucked, how no one liked you, and how things would not get better? These are all lies your negative brain has decided are true.

It is now time for you to begin finding the truth in those lies.

You can do this by looking for cold, hard evidence to combat the lies your brain is telling yourself. Going back to our earlier example, this could be by looking at the recordings or photos of you performing your hobby to show how you are actually getting better. Or, to start asking your friends to record your improvements. There is nothing like going over your past and present videos to see progress and how things are getting better or going in the direction you want.

Other options are screenshotting positive messages from clients, friends, or peers, writing down body measurements, or even asking loved ones to record quick little messages you can keep on your phone about how they will always be there for you and love you.

The goal here is to have any kind of hard truth to prove to your brain that you are wrong.

Positive Replacement

This is where things can sometimes become a little tricky. Replacing a negative with a positive in your overthinking mental cycle is a good thing, but you have to be able to do it realistically. Lying to yourself, even if it is with a positive twist, or not allowing your negative emotions to be acknowledged and validated, is really just replacing a negative cycle with this incredibly whacked out positive cycle. Which is not what you want. Have you ever been in a stressful situation where you are definitely not really positive, but you somehow manage to go, "It's fine, t'll all be okay," with a positive voice, which, if we are being honest, was probably more sarcasm than actual fact? That is not what we are aiming for here.

Coming up with positive replacements is not going to be easy, especially since your brain is probably going to treat anything positive like a foreign object which must be destroyed. It is going to take a concentrated effort for you to introduce this particular step, but it is incredibly worth it and necessary for you to do. That being said, there are two main ways to begin implementing positive replacements in your mind. You can either begin replacing with a more neutral truth that acknowledges the negative but enables a positive potential, or insert forms of sincere gratitude.

Neutral Truth

When using the neutral truth method, you are essentially replacing the blatant negativity of your mind by acknowledging the negativity and then bringing up an argument to stop the defeatism which is beginning to pop up.

For example: Perhaps you have begun to use negativity to isolate yourself from your social circles, with the lie that you did not enjoy yourself and no one wants you there. A neutral truth to the statement would be something like reminding yourself that you did have a good time while you were there, even though it took you a while to warm up to the atmosphere, and that your friends were glad you came.

In this example, you acknowledge that there were moments of awkwardness, but you began to reframe the context of your negativity by stating obvious facts, as well as memories and feelings that your brain is ignoring when pushing your negativity spiral. The truth you feed yourself is the actual truth, but it is neutral enough that your brain is able to tolerate its existence, while having the dual effect of beginning to stop the negative spiral.

The problem with neutral truths is that they can be easily used to continue the negative spiral, rather than as the stopping force. When you enact this solution, you need to make sure that the neutral truths are strong enough to force your brain to stop being negative, even for a few minutes. Unfortunately, finding a universal example of this is a little tricky, since these neutral truths need to deal with you and that particular negative spiral; making the best way to use this method as a trial and error type of situation. The good news is, once you find the type of neutral truths that work for your brain, you will be able to easily employ them in the future.

Sincere Gratitude

Finding things to be grateful for can be a struggle, especially when we are not in a good place. Yet there is no denying that even acknowledging the simplest things to be grateful for, like: you are alive, you are breathing, the sun is shining, it is the perfect weather, etc., can go a long way in helping you reframe your mind (Lang, 2018). All you need is that one tiny thing. It may seem completely redundant or unnecessary, or may even seem really silly to be grateful for. But do not let that fool you. All you need is that one tiny little thing.

Here's the catch, though. This has to be real and sincere gratitude. It cannot be snarky, sarcastic, or based off of someone's ill-fortune or bad day. What you are grateful for has to solely do with you, and has to be something actually pleasant. The difference between these two things is often what messes people up when they attempt to employ this particular solution.

Being grateful that you are not the loser, or the one who is in worse shape, definitely has its benefits; but at the end of the day it is really like comparing two negatives and hoping for a positive. While that might work for math and algebraic problems, that is not how it works in the real world (most of the time; there may be the odd scenario which will be unique to you and what is happening around you). You need to be sincerely grateful for that one thing in your life, and that thing has to be something which is actually positive. The good news is that the sincerity and gratefulness you feel can be small at first. If you are out of practice in how to apply gratitude in your life, being one thousand percent, sincerely grateful, may feel fake, and almost like you are pushing too hard.

In this context, the sincerity we are looking for is the tiniest bit of relief you feel when you acknowledge that one thing in your day, week, month, year, or scenario has gone right. It could even be that you got to see a sunset on a really bad day.

Setting Realistic Goals

Setting realistic goals may seem like an odd thing to tack onto the end of explaining how to dump negativity, so here is the logic. Overthinking is a habit, and the goal of this book and overcoming your overthinking is to replace it with better and more productive habits for your brain and life. Just like when we are actually building a habit, replacing one follows the same guiding principles of consistency, taking small steps, and being realistic and understanding of yourself and your situations to ensure success.

Therefore, fighting your overthinking brain and dumping negativity with your own brand of realism, truth, and positivity, is going to require the exact same work as installing a new habit into your life. You already know how to do all of the other steps, and you most likely even know how to set a realistic goal. However, this section is more so a caution than an explanation.

Overthinking has designed your brain to constantly think poorly of yourself and your abilities. This can manifest in either making unrealistic expectations (perfectionism) and setting yourself up to fail, or not even trying because you are too afraid to (analysis paralysis). In either scenario, your ability and knowledge to begin setting realistic goals in your life, and, in how to insert and use neutral truths and positivity to combat your brain's instinct, will be crucial for being successful.

An example of a realistic goal in regards to dumping negativity could be that you want to spend the next month paying attention to neutral truths you could insert into negative spirals. This is a small, but drastic enough, step to help you start in the right direction.

Set yourself up for success. Start small, plan more, dream large.

The Actual Steps

Dumping your negativity cycle can also be called a brain dump, and it essentially will force you to take everything which is residing in your brain during an overthinking and negative cycle, and begin to tear them apart and confront them. In this section, we are going to summarize and put everything that has been discussed into actionable steps you can begin doing today, to start your journey on stopping overthinking. These steps are going to overlap with some of the previous sections, but thanks to the help of Ronald L. Banks, there are going to be a few twists and new steps added in (Banks, 2020).

Dump It

As with the above section, take everything in your brain and dump it somewhere physical. This could be a journal, voice memo, your phone, computer, tablet, whatever is easier for you. When you are dumping everything out, do not even try to sort or analyze what is going on. Just literally take every thought, emotion, and what is going on around and in you and put it on the page (Banks, 2020).

Sort It

Now comes the fun new stuff: Sort out every thought that you just wrote down. There are three categories you can put them into: general thoughts, actionable items, and emotions or feelings. Once you have written them down, read through them and begin to ask yourself what is actually important right now, or how much you will care about this later on. Asking yourself these questions will begin to bring in perspective and awareness, while also helping you acknowledge and feel your feelings without spiraling.

For instance, if you have a thought that says, "I am frustrated at this event," you read it and log it as an emotion, and then ask yourself how important that particular feeling is right now. You have the option of saying it is really important, or not really that important in hindsight. Either answer acknowledges the emotion, and will also begin to guide you on what to do about it (such as acting on the emotion or acknowledging it and then letting it go) (Banks, 2020).

Change Your View of Fear

Fear is something we steer away from, and sometimes that is a good thing. Fear is healthy, and it is a signal from our brain telling us when something is wrong, or needs to be avoided. Yet so often we use the tiniest bit of fear as a reason to not continue, or to not grow and change our boundaries, perspectives, or situations.

Think about it for a moment. Every new beginning you have ever had most likely had the tiniest bit of fear in it. Going to university, or college. Starting a new school. Starting a new job. Beginning that new relationship. Moving to a different apartment or town. Getting married. Entering a committed relationship. Every single one of these big moments probably had some fear in it. You most likely got through most of those situations okay. You fought that fear, won, and grew as a person. We need to stop avoiding all fear and discomfort, because it is in those areas where we see who we are and what we are capable of, and are where we grow. That is not to say we cannot acknowledge when we are uncomfortable, or adapt to make our fears easier to go through; the key is to acknowledge our fear, assess how dangerous it is, and if we should fight it (and in regards to overthinking, you really should) and then press onward.

We Cannot Predict the Future

Until science really catches up to some sci-fi movies, we are pretty much stuck admitting that we cannot predict the future (or at least, that most of us cannot, if you believe in that type of stuff). What this means for your overthinking brain is that every type of analysis paralysis and fear you feel in regards to the future is essentially just over-worrying, and is causing more stress and anxiety than you need.

Please note that this is not the same as evaluating the consequences of certain actions and making grounded decisions based off of those results.

What we are discussing here is you not doing something because you do not know if it will be a good outcome. Or, not changing because you are scared of what could happen. Being scared of the unknown is okay. Being scared of the future is okay. Letting the fear and lack of knowledge control you is not. Start to fight these fears by rationalizing through them. Journal your thoughts, your fears, and your true emotions. Acknowledge that if you want your future to be different, you have to look at the present and past you. What did you do to become who you are now? What do you need to change?

Stop Waiting for Perfection

As has been mentioned before, perfection is not always possible, and it has become a crutch. Wanting to be perfect, or waiting until everything is perfect, is a good way to let your overthinking brain win and to not change. Do not let it do that to you anymore. You are not going to like reading this, but nothing will ever be the level of perfection that you are waiting for to do whatever it is you need to do.

Control Your Emotions

Ah, so we are back at controlling our emotions. This is an incredibly tricky step, because it is going to require you actually battling your current emotions and thought patterns. Thankfully, as mentioned previously, controlling your emotions does not mean ignoring what you feel or why. It means you have to acknowledge your emotions and begin to come up with solutions to fix or solve them.

Visualize What Can Go Right

Another great word for this is 'manifesting.' Starting your day with a manifestation of what could go right in your day—and then finding a way to put these reminders directly in your face or visual sphere—for the rest of the day, will help combat your overthinking and negative mind. Yes, it really is that easy. By focusing on what could go right, you will be too busy retraining your brain to let overthinking latch on, or stay attached to your mental pathways of negativity.

Summary

Honestly, negativity sucks. It is absolutely awful and no fun in how it creeps into every part of our lives with no warning or care for what it is actually doing to our confidence, abilities, and even ways of life. What's worse is that our brain seems to naturally latch onto this negativity, even though it knows that this type of thinking is bad for us. It is so, so much easier to do than to constantly fight it.

But fighting it will bring you the life and the change you want. If you want to be successful in combating your overthinking, you need to start dumping the negativity in your life, particularly the negative spirals your overthinking tends to cause. Thankfully, negativity cycles are short and only have two steps, meaning that your ability to: analyze, find the truth, introduce positive replacement through neutral truths or sincere gratitude, and setting realistic goals, are perfectly within your grasp. You simply have to start.

Which is easier said than done.

Reminder

This entire book is written with the up-beat, positive vibes of encouragement to help you jump-start your actual journey in fighting overthinking. However, there is also the fine line between drinking the Kool-Aid of all the 'you can do it!' statements in this book, and understanding the fundamental fact that we are all human. It would be lovely if you could simply read this book and instantaneously fix and stop your overthinking. It is not that easy. You need to allow yourself to make mistakes, otherwise you are actually going to give your overthinking and negative brain a reason to not continue on this journey.

Now, is it for sure that you will fail on your first go-round? No. No one knows for certain, because it is up to you. This is merely a reminder that you need to give yourself the ability to be human and make mistakes, while also having the determination and follow-through to continue trying.

Journal

Alright, so, for this chapter take your journal and begin to think of ways that you can begin fighting and dumping your negativity.

Start off with trying to remember the last time you negatively spiraled (if you have not journaled one out already), and try to think of common elements to those spirals. What are the similarities?

Once you have those similarities, begin to analyze them and come up with truths you can use to combat them in the future.

Next, pick which type of positive replacement you want to start with first. Come up with a few reminders or gratitude-isms you can put either in a calendar, phone, or in your notebook to look at throughout the day and remind yourself of them before your negativity spirals out of control.

Then, begin to set realistic goals for yourself incorporating everything you have learned so far (this will also be repeated at the end of the book).

Finally, write down the 'why's' of why you want to do this. These reasons will be your reminder when the going gets tough, as well as help become a sort of progress marker. These 'why's' are really the reasons you are doing this, and the more you combat and overcome your overthinking, the more you will be able to answer and solve those 'why's.; Having a record of that will be incredibly rewarding, as well as become a new incentive to stick with it.

CHAPTER 6

Life-Changing Practices to Stop Overthinking

And at long last, it is time to start going over more daily practical ways you can start to stop your overthinking tendencies. This chapter will build on the principles, guidelines, and mental discussions we have had so far. Meaning, that it will be assumed you are already working on certain things, and what will be recommended for you here, will specifically discuss new and different techniques which will hopefully be able to work in sync with everything else so far. The key for each of these recommended practices is not only for you to be able to use them immediately, but for you to have options for every type of overthinking your brain decides to pursue. If one tactic does not work for you, try another; or if you know one tactic will work for one type of overthinking compared to another, utilize that to your advantage.

Regardless of where you are in your overthinking journey, these practices will be incredibly beneficial to you, and it is highly recommended that you start them immediately.

Practices to Stop Overthinking Forever

Down to business. Each of these sections will contain steps, tricks, and ideas on how to stop your overthinking brain, as well as building suggestions, and 'end goals.' These suggestions will be meant for you to return to once you have gained consistency within each individual practice. The 'end goals' are really just a picture of what this practice will look like in regards to you and your overthinking over a long period of time.

Pace Yourself

At the risk of sounding repetitive: The very first thing you should do is pace yourself. No, this is not a green light to stop reading this book, or to slow down the momentum you have been building while reading this book.

Instead, remember that change does not happen overnight. You are taking on a long and tiring endeavor, because you are now going to go toe-to-toe with yourself, which can be guaranteed to be a pretty heated and hard-earned victory when you win. Be strategic. No one knows yourself better than you, outside of maybe a parent or safe person (they will be more aware of your idiosyncrasies than you probably are, unless you are incredibly self-aware); meaning, that you are most likely already aware of any types of self-sabotaging behaviors you may try to use to stop this journey. Not because you do not want to change, but because this change is going to mean confronting past demons you may actually prefer to ignore, or that you are afraid of what will come.

Yes, you need, and should, fight that fear; but do it wisely. Pace yourself. Set realistic goals, and let yourself be human and maybe fail (which, actually, is a great way to combat your overthinking brain, because you will be fighting your fear of change and confronting your need for perfection).

Pacing yourself is going to look different for everyone, so do not compare yourself to another person's journey. Use your newfound knowledge of awareness and cognitive replacement from the previous chapters to begin recognizing your self-sabotaging thoughts and to begin building actionable and realistic solutions to combat it.

Building

When it comes to pacing yourself, a great way to build on it is to actually continue on with it, and let it build with you. Sometimes, when we have paced ourselves for so long and then suddenly let go, our brains bounce back into this weird realm of, "Finally, I can go back to what I did before!" which is actually not what we want. Similar to implementing a new fitness routine or eating habit, pacing yourself can grow with you and your goals; and this growth will feel relatively natural to you. Chances are, if you pace yourself correctly, you will not even realize when you have scaled it to meet your newfound growth.

End Goal

The end goal of pacing yourself is to build a newfound self-awareness of what you are capable of, and how you will be able to get there. Instead of either expecting to be perfect the first go-round, or to look at something and just say, "someday," and never have a plan to get there, you will have found that perfect middle ground. You know what you want, how to get there, and how to ensure that your brain and body stay consistent to accomplish that goal.

Solutions

Which brings us to the next practice you can incorporate: problem solving. Yes, sadly, that particular math problem from elementary school is actually a life trait we all need to be able to use. However, we are not going to ask you how many oranges Susie has if she left Tennessee at 60 miles per hour. Instead, we are going to get personal.

Ask yourself these questions:

- Why do you not solve some of your problems (the easy ones, not the traumatic or deep-rooted ones)?

- What is your natural tendency to solve problems, if your overthinking brain was not in the way?

- What is the one way other people solve problems that drives you absolutely nuts?

Now, look at your answers and see if there is a general pattern you recognize about yourself. It could be that you do not want to problem solve because you are terrified to do so, you do not want to get into a conflict based on past experiences, or you have done it too quickly in the past and it did not end well. Whatever your reason or pattern, it is time to begin confronting that, because your overthinking brain will actually begin to slow down if you confront its downward spiral with a solution.

So how do you actually find a solution?

Turn your problem into a question. Asking yourself a question is a great way to begin jump-starting or remind your brain that you actually need to solve this problem, while also beginning to perhaps have alternate forms of thinking start in your brain.

Utilizing this method will actually begin to work on several past action we discussed, specifically: using the right perspective, inserting positive or neutral thoughts, and analyzing and sorting out your negativity and assigning it an action.

Building

As you build your solutions ability, you may not need to necessarily turn your problems into a question to begin thinking outside of the box. Again, this will most likely feel relatively more natural over time, because you will have trained your brain to look for actionable solutions rather than getting defeated or finding the solution which will not help you achieve what you want.

End Goal

The end goal of solution-making is to be able to take your overthinking, break it down, and come up with healthy and actionable solutions to it.

Journaling

Journaling is a great way to begin gaining a new perspective on solutions. It is amazing how different things can seem when we are able to distance ourselves from our problems, thoughts, and emotions by putting them onto paper, a screen, or into a voice memo. In fact, you have most likely been utilizing this method throughout the entire book so far. So, now, take a moment and look back at your first journal entries to the one for the last chapter. How do you feel from all those different thoughts on paper? Are you still emotionally attached to them, or have you been able to distance yourself to find better ways to think?

Part of the reason we fixate so easily when we overthink is because there is nothing to stop us from noticing our actual thoughts and emotions. Our mind becomes this thing of its own, and it feels like we are just along for the ride. Journaling out your thoughts and emotions —

especially while overthinking—will stop that.

It may not seem incredibly realistic to journal at the exact moment your brain starts to spiral out of control. What if it happens while you are in a meeting at work, or while you are in a fight with a loved one or colleague? You may not be able to journal right away, but since your brain is an overthinking brain, those thoughts and emotions are not going anywhere.

Begin to build the habit and discipline of bringing your journal with you everywhere, and make sure that you are able to find a quiet place to journal out your thoughts and feelings after the event, if you are unable to stop it immediately and begin journaling then. No matter when you journal out your problems, you are going to stop overthinking. Even if it is an hour or two after (although that is not ideal, but such is life).

The point of journaling is to remind your brain of the reality of the situation and to acknowledge your thoughts, but also to begin to distance yourself from them. This does not really have a time requirement, but this is also not the sign to journal only when you feel like it, when it is convenient, or to not journal altogether.

You may not like it, but you need something to distance yourself from your thoughts, and journaling will provide you with that ability.

Building

After journaling out your thoughts, as discussed in the previous chapter, you have a choice. You can either make actionable steps off of those emotions you are now re-reading, or you can ignore them. However, ignoring your feelings has to actually be because you are able and okay to ignore them. You cannot just simply disregard them because they are too much work or effort to deal with, or the actionable step they are pointing you towards is too much work (realistically, you can do that, but then you are not going to stop your overthinking patterns). Actionable steps are scary, and that is completely natural and normal to feel; but if you let that fear control you, then you are going to read this book and not be any different.

Similarly, you cannot use your journal as a crutch. Just because you journal and feel better does not mean that you can stop a conversation mid-way and journal right then and there. There are appropriate times and places to journal and put your feelings to paper, and you have to be aware of those.

Over time, you may realize that you do not need to journal as much as when you originally started this journey, because your brain has developed the ability of finding perspective within itself naturally and easily. This is actually possible, but it takes a lot of training and accountability to get there.

End Goal

The end goal of journaling—whether you actually keep this habit or not—is to help you find new ways to gain perspective and organize your thoughts as they come to you.

Meditation

Meditation is not just for yoga enthusiasts, it is for anyone who needs a moment and the space to breathe and distance themselves from their environments in a positive way. When it comes to overthinking, one of the best ways to meditate is to actually combine meditation, which is emptying your mind and focusing only on your breath, with mindfulness which is simply to just fixate on what you are doing. Nothing else. If you are folding laundry, just fold laundry. Do not let your brain begin to wander or think about all the negative things that it would like to, and do not fixate on the triggering event which caused the downward spiral. The key is to focus on the mundane and routine. This focus will stop your negative spiral, while also allowing those emotions to slowly drain out of you (also known as, you guessed it, gaining distance from your emotions to begin building your perspective).

Or, if that does not work for you, you can use the more yoga-esque way of meditating. Find a quiet place, sit still, and focus on your heartbeat and your breath. Slowly let your thoughts and emotions drain out of you, and only focus on your body. These actions will do the same thing as focusing on a mundane and routine task.

For the record, it is very well acknowledged how hard this is. Our overthinking brains are trained to think at top speed all the time, and our society and work lives have not made that any easier. Something is always happening, lists always need to be made, and emotions always need to be felt, validated, and acted on. Taking the time, energy, and even having the ability to let that all go and just focus on that one particular thing is going to be hard.

But you can do it.

Building

Building meditation really depends on what you are using it for, and how you do it. If you are using meditation to simply empty your mind to gain perspective, then you could build in such a way as to get to that place of blessed peace and neutrality more quickly. However, if you decide to tack on other things to meditation, such as using that as a quiet time to begin retraining your brain, or to implement new positive thoughts into your head, you could begin building or scaling how long you meditate per day, or how often.

End Goal

The end goal of meditation is different for everyone, because it has so many different benefits and possibilities. A great general end goal of meditation is being able to sink into that mindset easily and not be too worried about your surroundings or the necessary aids you needed previously to get there.

Distractions

This one may seem like a contradiction, considering that the last practice was about emptying your mind and only focusing on one thing to begin gaining perspective on your emotions. However, there are some days where that is honestly just not possible. Our thoughts, feelings, and emotions are this constant buzzing in the back of our heads that never goes away, like that annoying fly at a picnic.

If that is happening to you, find gentle and soothing distractions you can use to begin getting your brain to focus on anything other than the negative spiral it is insisting on. This could be something like: taking a hot shower, going for a walk, reading a book, listening to music, dancing, talking to a friend, or even going into nature. Anything that provides a physical or mental space to let your brain begin to calm down (Welle (www.dw.com), 2020).

The key with these distractions is that they distract you enough to gain distance from your overthinking, but not to the point where you forget and are unable to return to those thoughts. You may not really want to but you need to return to these thoughts, because if they are nagging at you so badly where you are unable to meditate; your brain is most likely bringing to the surface something you actually need to pay attention to and address.

Building

Building this particular practice can go two ways. Either you are able to shorten the length of the distraction to gain perspective more quickly and bring about a resolution sooner, or, you are able to build this practice to the point where you address your overthinking with a calm or happy mind (depending on your situation).

End Goal

Honestly, the end goal for distracting yourself is actually to find the distraction(s) that work for you. There are going to be messy situations in this life, ones where we will need some type of self-soothing that is healthy and proactive, to help us find a place of peace and resolution. Finding one, or several, methods that you know will work for you, could do wonders as you go forward in life. In regards to overthinking, this practice will hopefully help you feel more capable in beginning to tackle and stop your overthinking tendencies.

Small Note

Remember way back in the introduction where we discussed the brain. Your environment is going to play a big factor in what you are able and willing to do when it comes to fighting your overthinking brain. This is especially important in this note because you are looking for healthy and peaceful distractions to help your brain distance itself from overthinking and begin to positively combat it. Being in a negative environment is not going to really help you proactively create that (if at all).

Pay special attention to your environment in regards to your distractions. If you pick a negative distraction (even if it is negative music) you may not notice the same positive effects you were aiming for.

If you are looking for ways to help this, here are a few quick tips (which are going to sound pretty similar to some other sections of this book, but bear with it for now). First, stop putting the wrong things in. This means being aware that something is negatively affecting you, and intentionally trying to stop using, going, or being there. Second, start putting the right thing in (or, begin to use positive replacement). Third, get the things that should not be there, out. Essentially, anything that is helping or continuing your negative mindsets should be addressed. If it is a relationship, ask the other person if they would be willing to attempt being more positive with you. If it is a workplace issue, begin to think about how you could make it more positive, or look for ways to change positions. If it is your living environment, begin to think of ways that you can safely make it more positive for you.

Yes, this is going to be a lot of work in and of itself, but it will be worth it. A positive environment will encourage a positive mindset, which will continue to encourage you to combat your overthinking tendencies.

However

If something is negative to the point where it is dangerous or toxic for you to be there, find a safe person to help you get out immediately.

Journal

Now that we are at the end of this book, begin to think about what you could actually start doing today, tomorrow, or this week.

Remember, Rome was not built in a day, and it is certainly not assumed that you will be able to beat your overthinking in a short timespan either, so let's just take that option right off the table. With time, diligence, and outside support through a mentor, safe person, or licensed therapist, you will be able to do this, but it will take time. So, now that you have been forced to acknowledge that this is going to be a long process, start to break down what you could do from this chapter immediately and how you are going to build on it.

So, which one of these practices do you think you could reasonably begin to incorporate daily?

How are you going to incorporate it?

How are you going to ensure that you continue to incorporate it when the going gets tough? (How are you going to stay accountable?)

Keep this journal with you as you begin to build and reach the end goal of these practices, return to these first day pages to see how you have scaled things and begun to figure out how your brain works. This type of personal insight will be invaluable in creating a healthier and stronger mind in combating your overthinking.

Conclusion

So we have come to the end of discussing how to combat your overthinking mind. We have gone over many things, so a few of the introductory things will be summarized and re-tied into the rest of what the book discussed, to help you begin to put everything together with a nice little metaphorical bow on top.

Overthinking is putting too much harmful thought into something. Even though our brain has fallen for the trap of believing this type of thinking is productive, it is not, and most likely never will be. When our brains overthink, they tend to concentrate on worrying, rumination, obsession, or anxiety-driven types of thoughts. Overthinking can present itself in two main ways: we are either worrying about the past, or are worrying about the future. We have continued to get away with this type of thinking because people have not called us out on it, we have convinced ourselves and everyone around us that it is productive thinking, or, we have done it for so long we are no longer fully aware of what we are doing. Regardless of how we got here, we are actively combatting brains that most likely have months, if not years, of ingrained negative behavior patterns.

These patterns are the habit of overthinking, which have to be replaced with new, positive habits. Remember: Nature abhors a vacuum, and getting rid of overthinking without putting something in its place would create a mental vacuum that we should not leave empty if our brain is ill-prepared to handle it. Without the proper hard work and determination, stopping overthinking will most likely just open your brain up to another bad habit, and we are back to where we started (but with a different book title).

Additionally, our habit of overthinking is most likely prompted and continued by living in a perpetual form of stress, which, in turn, has the potential to alter our brain's functionality and actual brain chemistry. Prolonged exposure to stress has potentially incredibly bad results for our brain; it can stop our fear center, as well as limit our brain's ability to learn, be social, and control the stress hormone of cortisol (TED-Ed, 2015).

But that is just what overthinking through stress does to our brains physically and chemically. When it comes to our actual mind, overthinking has a deeper and more problematic result. Remember: Our mind and our brain are two different parts of the same thing. Every thought we have enters our mind, which then begins to create neural pathways in our brain. These neural pathways encode every part of our thought, from the triggering action, to the actual thought, to our surrounding emotions and reactions. Additionally, the more those particular neural pathways are traveled, the stronger those pathways become. Meaning, that the more we continue down a negative mental path, the stronger those emotions and pathways become. When we consistently think negatively, like when we overthink, we are literally building stronger forms of negativity into our minds and brains through constant use of those neural pathways (Leaf, 2019).

Thankfully, your brain is able to bounce back and fix itself (TEDx Talks, 2020a). This is where all of the techniques and practices we have liscussed come in. By finding ways to strengthen new neural pathways ind replace old ones, you can overcome overthinking. However, you need to set yourself up for success. This includes being consistent, asking for help when you need it, and ensuring that you are allowing yourself to both succeed and fail.

While it may seem odd, if you do not allow yourself to have the potential to fail on this journey, you will actually fail. Why? Because putting in that mental wall of not letting yourself fail, you are actually continuing an overthinking tendency of perfectionism. Allowing yourself to fail is actively combatting that need for perfection while simultaneously giving yourself learning opportunities to find what ways work best for you in fighting your overthinking tendencies.

Also, remember that overthinking is not a form of problem solving or self-reflection. Overthinking's inherent negative attitudes make sure that nothing productive comes out of those types of thoughts; meaning, that you will never be able to properly solve or reflect on anything when you are in that mental state.

By now you have hopefully been journaling for a few days and have begun to develop some introspective tendencies towards your overthinking brain and its peculiarities. Gaining these new insights about yourself may feel and seem defeating, but try to not let them get to you. You need to understand how your brain and overthinking is working in order to fully stop that particular habit, and this includes acknowledging some of the messy and not great sides to ourselves.

Just remember: Many people have been where you are, and have fought the same fight you are fighting. You are not alone in this, you are worthy of not thinking this way, and you are capable of doing it.

Also, do not be afraid or ashamed to reach out to someone, whether that be a safe person or a professional, to ask for help if you need to. Think of this journey like an elimination diet. It will be long, you may have a few tiny mess-ups, but hopefully, by the time you are finished with this journey, you will be more self-aware and able to tackle the things which caused you to stumble and mess up in the past.

You got this.

Thank You

Before you leave, I'd just like to say, thank you so much for purchasing my book.

I spent many days and nights working on this book so I could finally put this in your hands.

So, before you leave, I'd like to ask you a small favor.

Would you please consider posting a review on the platform? Your reviews are one of the best ways to support indie authors like me, and every review counts.

Your feedback will allow me to continue writing books just like this one, so let me know if you enjoyed it and why. I read every review and I would love to hear from you. Simply visit the link below to leave a review.

Printed in Great Britain
by Amazon

23819316R00158